What people say about Nick James

W9-BNS-290

"Nick James is a true inspiration to every business owner or budding new entrepreneur. It's no surprise that recently Nick won 'Internet Marketer Of The Year' as voted for by over 200 other business leaders and full-time marketers.

What he teaches simply works, and he has a wonderful way of explaining how you can implement his ideas quickly and simply"

**Matt Bacak,
MattBacak.com**

Nick's new book 'Six Figures a Year in Info Publishing' is a complete roadmap for anyone wanting to start their own business in this wonderful world of Info Publishing. If you're looking for the 'secret to success' online then I recommend you read this book cover to cover, pen in hand and then follow his plan.

**Neil Stafford
TheTrainingVault.com**

"Nick's marketing methods are truly inspirational. You can't go far wrong if you stick to these principles and strategies, which is exactly why I believe you should read this book from cover to cover."

**Clate Mask
Infusionsoft.com**

First Printing: 2018

Printed in the U.S.A.

Contents

Your EXTRA Bonuses!

I really want to give you everything I can to help you set up your new $100k a year business, so I've created a very special free download package of extra goodies just for you.

This bonus package includes 11 quick and easy-to-read reports. In total there are 340 tips, more than 137 pages, of solid meaty, useful and practical information with one aim in mind: to help you to set up your new business for maximum profit in minimum time.

The information in the reports is priceless and could be responsible for literally hundreds of thousands of extra dollars in sales heading your way over the next 10 years.

Simply Text The Word **FREEGIFTS** To
+1 (702) 919 6146
Now For Download Instructions.

Acknowledgements

There are so many people I want to thank for being willing to share their ideas, thoughts and philosophies with me. These have all contributed to both my own entrepreneurial success in this fantastic high speed direct marketing world in which we live... and also contributed to the thoughts presented to you in this book. I also want to thank my wife and business partner Kate and the dedicated team who help me to implement hundreds of ideas each year, creating new products, marketing materials, tracking campaigns, split testing, and studying the results to ultimately find out what works.

Of course what works is what I've written about extensively within the pages of this very book, and it's my pleasure to be able to share these strategies with you.

While there are many, many business leaders, authors, entrepreneurs and thinkers whom I have learned from over the years, there are a special few who have made a significant impact on my entrepreneurial success.

Stuart Goldsmith for first opening my mind with his best-selling book The Midas Method, Robert Kiyosaki for explaining to me his The Cash Flow Quadrant philosophy, Andrew Reynolds for introducing me to the world of 'Cash On Demand' and marketing using traditional Direct Mail campaigns, Matt Bacak for taking me under his wing and teaching me so much about email marketing and split testing, Tom Cone at MemberGate.com for inspiring me to build my first ever online community and to test out a continuity business model, Kevin Polly at arpReach.com for his never-ending enthusiasm, support and knowledge in helping me to get my email marketing delivered, Christopher John Payne for his help and encouragement in creating and publishing this book, and also to Clate Mask for creating the wonderful Infusionsoft which has become such a highly valued part of our business.

Last, and by no means least, I would like to thank you, my customer. It is my desire to help you to achieve as many of your business endeavours as I can. That's what gets me fired up and excited each and every day. As Warren Buffet has previously said, "I love the process more than the proceeds". It's the questions and feedback that I've often received from customers that's helped me to identify new product opportunities and for this I am ever grateful to you.

About the Author

Nick James has built 3 separate million dollar a year internet businesses since his Entrepreneurial journey began in 2001.

Nick is a true example of a self-made success and it's his own personal experience that make him understanding and approachable on all business levels, working with enthusiastic entrepreneurs at varying stages of their journey into business.

Business coach, mentor, software developer, internet marketing expert – Nick James won 'Internet Marketer of the year' 2016-2017 and continues to turn heads with his direct marketing ideas.

Nick is also a 'Global Angel' and is actively involved in various fund-raising activities for the international **Global Angels Charity**, raising funds to empower children, young people and their communities whether they are living in extreme poverty or disadvantage, devastated environmental conditions, with disability or life threatening illness, are street kids, orphans, child slaves, trafficked kids, or child soldiers.

Websites:

       www.Nick-James.com
       www.InternetMarketingTrainingClub.com

1

My goal and yours:
$100,000 extra a year

My name is **Nick James**, and my one goal in writing this book is to help put more money into your bank account. Money that you've been missing out on, and losing out on, from one of the most lucrative, most untapped, most incredible opportunities of your entire life.

What is that opportunity I hear you ask. It's the ability to quickly and easily start your own business. However not just any business. A business that can be started on a shoe string budget and stacked in your advantage from the very beginning. The business is called *Info Publishing*.

Would that be helpful for you?

I want to make sure you stop losing out on hundreds of thousands of dollars, maybe much more - money you may not even realise you are losing out on simply because you're too busy 'working' for a living.

Four Things I Want You To Know

First, I want to share with you my own story, of how I went from being a broke entrepreneur, living on a minimal wage, living in a run-down home in the worst part of town, to making *millions of dollars* per year from a small collection of simple websites selling info products.

First making 5 figures, then 6 figures, and then eventually 7 figures a year.

Do you think you could get by if I gave you another *6* figures?

How about if I gave you another *7* figures?

You can pay some bills with that, right?

Second, I want you to know about **5 Myths** you've been led to believe (by others) that are holding you back from running your own highly profitable *6 Figures A Year* online business, which *you may not even know* are holding you back.

The third thing I want to explain is why the Info Publishing business is simply one of the very best businesses for the 'normal' person to have, compared to a 'traditional' business and how you can get set up virtually immediately, even today if you like.

The fourth thing I want to share with you is 4 simple, easy ways to **add $100,000 per year to your online Information Business, starting right now.**

2

My story

So this is how I went from a complete mess, to success. If you had been with me back in December 2000, you'd have seen me at the lowest point in my life.

No, I wasn't homeless and living under a bridge, or anything like that. But I'd just gone through a messy breakup. The relationship I'd been in for the previous 7 years had hit the rocks, in such a way that it meant I had to move out of the family home and effectively start all over again. I can tell you the most painful thing back then was not being able to read a bedtime story every night to my then 5-year-old son. It truly broke my heart.

This awful turn of events came about because, well, because I was always out working long hours, holding down a multitude of jobs on minimum wage.

Here's me standing outside the old Parking Lot where I worked for a minimum wage.

Trying to keep a roof over my family's head, I'd get up early in the morning. Literally, at the crack of dawn, I would leave the house and head to a

This old red van was my only vehicle even though I was working three jobs.

parking lot in the city center, where I'd work from 6 a.m. to 10 a.m. every weekday morning.

And then, after my shift finished, I'd get into my old red, rusty panel van and, for the rest of the day, deliver packages for a local courier company.

During evenings and weekends, I would work as a DJ until late into the night, playing music at various parties, especially in the run-up to the Christmas holiday period. Again, all in an effort to bring in some extra much-needed cash.

I did all of this under the impression that, to be a man, I had to work hard and earn as much money as I possibly could in order to do the best for my young family, to pay the mortgage, to pay the bills, and put food on the table.

However, the reality was that, in the end, I hardly ever saw my partner. We became like ships that pass in the night. I would be out working most of the time, and she would be at home, looking after our son.

One night I came home earlier than she expected. The Christmas party I was DJing at had finished early. And, well, let's just say my 5-year-old son wasn't the only man in the house when I got home that night.

She was having an affair.

I won't go into all the personal details and everything that happened following that particular moment but, needless to say, I started to question everything about my life. After all, I had been working my ass off, and this is how I was being treated.

Things had to change. I never, ever, wanted to go through anything like this again.

And things did change pretty quickly after that.

I remember it …

Hey, I know I'm in the middle of my story, but let me emphasize this: at the beginning of every presentation you do, whether it's a webinar or sales letter, it's important to tell your story because no one will ever really hear you until they know you. I wish someone had told me the importance of stories when I was first getting used to putting presentations together for my business.

Okay, back to my story.

I remember it happened one particular cold and wet morning soon after New Year's Day, when I was working outside at the parking lot.

A smartly dressed guy driving a very nice, brand new, BMW 7 Series car had found it boxed in by a truck and couldn't drive out.

Instead of getting angry with me, he asked to join me in my small office for a hot cup of coffee as we waited for the van driver to return so he could get on his way. As we made some small talk, I complimented him on his smart car and asked what he did for a living.

He told me he was an *information publisher*, which he went on to explain. Really it meant that what he did was to sell books, manuals, home study courses and cassette tapes, videotapes and DVDs by mail order (this was 17 years ago). Back then it was still the early days of the Internet, so instead of providing instant downloadable products he would simply ship everything out to his customers in the mail.

And judging by the $100,000 luxury car he was driving, he was doing very well with it. In fact, he told me that he had become a self-made millionaire in less than 5 years, thanks to his business.

He then asked about me, and I told him everything that had just happened to me at home.

What he said next I have never forgotten. In fact, this has been the *most valuable lesson* I have ever learned. Quite literally, **this one thing** has, over the years, turned into more than $16 million worth of advice. I'm not exaggerating, because that's how much money I have generated based on what he shared with me during that cup of coffee.

He explained to me that the model I was using to earn money and become better off financially was *seriously flawed*. That's why I'd found myself in a place where I never seemed to have enough time, or enough money, because I'd sold my effort to someone else at a discount.

He said, whenever someone says to you, "Give me some of your time, and I will give you some money," the answer should be "No." He said things will only change for you when you *stop exchanging time for money.*

It took a while for the profound wisdom he had just shared to sink in.

I was working 3 or 4 jobs at a time, always selling my time for money. The trouble was that every job I was doing paid minimum wage.

So it wasn't surprising that I was always tired and cranky, and, with a young family to house and feed, I'd never have any money left at the end of the month.

He went on to explain that his income was not linked to the number of hours in the day, or the number of hours he worked.

It was linked to the number of books, manuals and home study courses he sold, which he explained were cheap to produce and sold for considerable amounts.

A huge lightbulb went on in my imagination. I might have been working hard; I might have been working smart (or so I had thought at the time) ... but I was focused on the wrong income model entirely.

It was at about this moment that the owner of the truck that was boxing him in returned, and he had to leave.

But before he left, he did two things. First, he handed me his business card and said that if I was truly interested in what he did I should give him a call, and second, he handed me 3 videotapes from the trunk of his car. He told me they were a gift in return for the coffee he'd just had.

With that, he got in his car and drove off.

Later that night, when I eventually finished work and got back to the room I was renting, I watched all 3 of the 60-minute videotapes he had given me, back-to-back and twice over. My mind was racing with new possibilities. I had never even thought about anything like this before. In fact, I remember I found it extremely hard to get to sleep that night.

The following morning I picked up the phone and called the guy, worried as to whether he'd even remember me. It was during that call he invited me to attend a one-day master class he was planning the following week, where he was preparing to teach his unique business system to a select group of specially invited guests. It wasn't cheap. A couple of grand, if I remember correctly. However, investing that money in myself and learning his system was the best thing I've ever done for myself.

I've not looked back since, and boy, have things changed for me. I just did what he showed me, and my own information publishing business took off like a rocket - just like he said it would...

Now, please don't get me wrong: I still work hard. I guess it's just in my nature. However, I only work for about 3 hours a day. And the rest of the time? Well, I met somebody new: the woman of my dreams. We're now happily married and settled down. We enjoy spending time together, either enjoying days out at the spa, or taking several vacations a year, or perhaps even heading out scuba diving with our son, Josh.

None of this would have been possible if I hadn't been told there was a different income model to follow and to *STOP selling your time for money* - and to start a business selling information-based products.

If you take nothing else away from this book, please remember this: things will only change for you, as they have for me, if you change your income model.

You can never "save" yourself rich. It's not surprising that most people with an above-average income run their own business, one NOT based on selling time for money. And likewise, it's not surprising that anyone with a job will only manage to get by, month-to-month. Even the highest paid attorneys and IT specialists still only have 24 hours in the day, like me and you. As we now both know, that model is flawed. Period.

It's only when you change the *model* that you'll begin to get out of the 9-to-5 rat race, like I did. Listen: It's not your fault. It's just unlikely that anyone has told you about this before now.

Okay, that's my story of how I went from a mess to a success. And I hope you can see just how valuable that *one lesson* I learned turned into a fortune - because there's no reason why it cannot do the same thing for you.

3

The 5 Myths

There are a few things you need to be on the lookout for, so your newfound entrepreneurial enthusiasm and efforts don't get sabotaged along the way, sometimes by others and sometimes by your own crooked thinking.

I mean by that the second thing I promised: to identify the 5 myths you've been led to believe by others that are holding you back from being successful with your new business.

Myth Number 1: Money is bad

I've had people tell me that it's not right that you "sell" your products. *Don't you remember you started with nothing? You should be putting everything you're doing online for free because you're all about "making a difference."*

I say: So what if you charge for your products? That doesn't mean you aren't still going to make a difference to someone's life when they read and put into practice your information and training.

You write checks for charities and donate online. You don't always volunteer your time. So watch out for that little jab that gets thrown at you from time to time.

I believe money allows you to give back, help others and *make a difference*. To date, my wife and I have personally raised and donated many tens of thousands of dollars to various charities like Global Angels, which is a 100% giving charity that helps children in Africa receive a proper education, clean drinking water, clothes and food. We also donate to Naomi House & Jack's Place in Hampshire, a hospice for life-limited and life-threatened children and young people.

How is money *bad* when you can contribute your bit to help young people go through extremely tough times in a little bit more comfort and with a little extra kindness?

Let me ask you a question: Do you believe in the products you sell? Do you believe in your business and what you are trying to do in the world? *Yes?*

Okay, question two: Do you believe your products will make a positive difference in the lives of others, or make the world a better place? *Yes?*

Then you're doing people a disservice by not getting your product or service into their hands.

If you really believe in your product, as you may now be thinking, and you know it helps people, then why wouldn't you do everything you can to ethically push them over the line to buy your product or to read your books so you can really have a major positive impact on somebody?

And hey, if you make a little money doing it, God bless. You should make money, because you're *running a business*.

When tropical storms and bad weather devastated the lives of people in the Caribbean and British Virgin Islands not so long ago, I was able to join forces with one of the biggest organizations of charitable givers in the world and write a check to contribute to the disaster relief fund. *So, how is money bad?*

If you're able to provide clean drinking water and put food in hungry people's bellies in Africa, *how in the heck can money be bad?*

If you care for your aging parents because they were so wonderful to you as a child growing up, and you are now taking care of them, or you're working to get yourself out of debt so you don't have to stress, *how is money bad?*

By the way, did you know more relationships and more marriages end because of financial issues than because of fidelity issues? If you look at the research, you'll discover that a financial issue often leads to other things.

So, think about that. All things considered, why wouldn't we focus on mastering the skill of making money?

The reason is we get pre-programmed by society to believe that money is bad, and a lot of times it's Hollywood that does this to us.

Let me explain. There is something called a *meme*. A meme is a virus of the mind. Just like a computer gets a virus, our minds get viruses, and if you don't clean your personal hard drive, you'll remain infected.

You start to get a poverty-conscious mindset, and here's what we have to understand...

- your thoughts will determine your feelings
- your feelings determine your beliefs
- your beliefs determine your habits
- your habits determine your actions
- your actions determine your results.

It all starts way back there with *how you think* and *what you put in your head*.

If you don't cultivate a garden, weeds are going to grow.

If you put bad fuel in your car, your car won't run properly.

If you put good gas in, it zooms along.

Okay, so Hollywood and television pre-program us with this virus of the mind, and we start to be pre-programmed with the belief that **money is bad**.

Have you ever watched the film *Titanic*? A great love story, huh? ☺

Actually, *one of the worst financial programming movies you could ever imagine!*

Let's play this out. Kate Winslet's character, Rose: she's with a billionaire, and yet she's so miserable. *Goldarn it, I cannot eat another steak and lobster. Right?*

She meets up with Jack (*ahh … Leonardo DeCaprio*).

The billionaire is all stuffy. The guys are smoking cigars, sipping brandy, eating lobster and steak, having such a miserable life.

However, Rose goes downstairs, down to the bottom deck of the ship, with Jack.

And what does she see? They're hooting and hollering, dancing on the tables and having fun! And what does one of them say to her? *We don't have much money, but at least we're happy.*

Subconsciously, we viewers are being programmed. Money = stuffy.

Who's always the bastard character in the movie? The rich guy or the rich lady?

Who's always the villain? The rich guy or the rich woman?

Who's always the hero? The heroine? The person we root for? *The poor person.*

We get programmed in our subconscious mind, just like a virus infecting us that tells us that money is bad, and then we start to sabotage our conscious entrepreneurial efforts with thoughts like:

"I don't want to make too much money, because people might start thinking that I'm a bad person."

So we start sabotaging our own success.

We stop marketing, we stop calling people back, we worry too much about being lumped into that category that's floating around out there.

It's in movies everywhere. The rich person is always the bad person. The poor person is always the hero. Another example: *Robin Hood Prince of Thieves.* ☺

My advice: Start watching movies differently. Just watch and see who the bad person is. It's always the person who's making a lot of money. And we don't even realize what's going on at such a deep subconscious level.

If you've studied how the mind works, you know that it absorbs images, and that the mind gets *pinged* in an unconscious state. And all that stuff just starts sinking in, sinking in, until all of a sudden that's who you become.

You start believing that way, and you start acting that way.

You've got to change those thoughts.

If you want different results from what you're currently getting, then you've got to change your thoughts, way back at the beginning of the cycle.

Remember: Thoughts determine feelings. Feelings determine your beliefs. Your beliefs determine your habits, your habits determine your actions, and your actions determine the results.

If you want to change the results, it starts with the thoughts you put in the beginning.

Okay? *So how can money be bad?* You've got to dispel the myth and look at the good stuff that you're able to do with money. Think of the people you're able to help. And if you want to help other people, then I believe this: you've got to help yourself first, before you can help others.

You've got to take care of *you*, and it's okay to do that. You're not a bad person if you do.

I know you want to give and serve and contribute back to society. We all do, really. So why is it not okay to take care of you? Make some money doing it. You should. You're running a business.

Myth Number 2: Think positive, follow your passion, do what you love, and the money will follow

Have you heard that one?

Yes? Well, let me tell you something. First of all, it's not about just having a positive attitude.

I can be positive all I want, but I will never be a jockey - *I'm too tall*. Okay, this is not going happen. You can think: *But I'm positive. I'm going to be a jockey. I'm going to be a jockey. I'm going to win the Derby.* It's still simply not going to happen.

It really doesn't matter how much positive thinking I have.

Listen, I'm not saying we shouldn't think positively, but what I want you to do is have a different mindset about your business.

You may be thinking: *What's wrong with following your passion?*

I'm not saying we shouldn't be passionate about what we're doing, but I regularly hear these self-help guru types say things like: *all you need is passion*, and I'm thinking: *Really? REALLY!*

So, you don't need to know how to run a business, then? You don't need to know how to create products or rebrand the ones you've licensed? Write ethical yet persuasive sales copy? Upsell to other products? Process payments, recruit joint venture partners, drive a never-ending supply of qualified leads to your website? Really? You don't need to know any of that stuff?

Come on. That's just not real.

While it might be a nice, politically correct thing to say - *"Just have passion, you're going to do okay, just go for it, give it a try"* - you need to have your tactical manoeuvres in place. You've got to have strong roots.

Then there's the conclusion: *"Do what you love and the money will follow."* Isn't there a book title like that? Sounds really cute.

So let me say this: The fact that you *love something* doesn't necessarily mean there is a market out there with enough money floating about to support your business. For example, you may have a real passion for underwater basket weaving; it might even be what you dream about doing every weekend. But if no one else happens to be interested, you're not going to remain in business for very long, no matter how passionate you are, or how creative your marketing is.

Myth Number 3: Selling is bad

I hear people all the time who say, *"Nick, I have the greatest product, I have the greatest message, I've got the best service. But I don't want to tell too many people about it, because I don't want them to think I'm trying to sell them something!"*

If you think this way, chances are that, again, there is a meme virus in your mind. You've been pre-programmed, subconsciously, to think salespeople (and selling) are bad. But listen: you have to sell; it's part of business. But I don't want it to seem like you're too pushy, either.

So here's what I want you to do. In your mind, cross off *selling is bad*, and instead write down *AME*. This is how you should always approach things. AME is:

A = Always add value
M = Make a difference
E = Enrich people's lives

After some 17 years selling online, I'm blessed to have become quite a good copywriter. That is, I have written mailing pieces and sales letters that have pulled in over **$16 million to date.** In fact, I've written two sales letters that have pulled in over $1 million each. And I've spoken about these sales letters many times at live workshops and events where I've been asked to speak.

However, when I get off stage, people at those seminars and events often come up and ask me, *"Nick, how can I write a sales letter that makes me a million dollars?"*

I tell them the first thing they need to know is this:

That you should never put together a product, service or a sales letter to simply make a million dollars. Instead, you should start with AME in mind.

Once you have worked out how you're going to

- Always add value
- Make a difference and
- Enrich people's lives

The rest becomes much, much easier. Because that gives everything balance.

You've got the wrong spirit from the beginning if you simply concentrate on what's in it for you.

That's the first thing I always tell them: Do we want to make sales? Of course. We all do. But you have to put a product offering together with the *primary aim* of:

- Adding value
- Make a difference, and
- Enrich people's lives

You see, when you buy a product from me - any product - **my primary goal** is that you have more useful information, more tips, more advice and more things that will help to catapult you toward the success goals you have set for yourself. More than anything else, it should give you everything you need.

That's my primary goal. And I think if you always create your products or your training that way, you will always be fine.

Of course, I hope you will buy other products from me. I *want* you to buy other products from me in the future. In fact, I hope you buy all my products. But all that is always *secondary* to *my primary goal*: to *AME*. (In other words, I don't just create a product with the goal of simply selling as many copies as I can.)

Once you've done that, it's time to begin writing a killer sales letter that will convince people to arrive at the inevitable conclusion that they want to buy your product.

You see, it will never feel like you're *selling* when you know in your heart that you have something special, something you honestly feel other people would be better off having in their lives. This is the cornerstone of my business philosophy.

Myth Number 4: You've tried it all before and it doesn't work

This is another thing you've been led to believe.

No doubt, you've probably tried a lot of ways, but you haven't tried the way you'll learn from me, which is *the right way*.

As I explained earlier, as I was telling you my story, you can work *hard* and you can even work *smart* ... or you can work *right*. It's not your fault that you haven't had a roaring success with your own business until now. You simply haven't found the *right way* yet, because you've been listening to people who've advised you on *outdated* or *incorrect* ways to do it.

Myth Number 5: Don't trust someone you haven't heard from before, or new ways of doing things

I don't blame you if you're skeptical. You shouldn't trust *anybody*. The fact is, if we haven't done business before, then you shouldn't trust me right off the bat. Let me *earn* your trust and prove it to you.

I've been online since July 4, 2001. That was before MySpace, before Google, before Facebook and before Twitter.

Right now, at our customer feedback site, mycustomercomments.com, our ratings average 4.97 out of 5 stars.

Plus, all of the digital products we sell online always include a full **30 days complete satisfaction money-back guarantee,** so first-time customers can order with confidence, safe in the knowledge that their purchase is completely risk-free.

Happy customers buy from us again and again. And each time they do that, it's via a secure website showing a "security padlock" in the browser.

Here are just a small handful of messages we've received from customers and clients over the years:

PAUL HOLLINS

"After attending one of Nick's events in 2012, I decided to meet up with him privately for a one-to-one coaching session. As a result of what Nick showed me, I now have a business which is pulling in a steady $12,000 each month via a very unique niche and have found customers wanting my services in nearly every corner of the globe. I now consider Nick to be more than a business coach and a very dear friend."

SARWAN SUMON

"Twelve months ago my business was disorganized and I was wasting too much time and effort on non-fee-earning tasks. I did not have a clear direction or strategy. The result of working with Nick: my income doubled within a year. Which has allowed me to choose when and where I work. I can even work from home if I want to. No commutes. No boss. No worries."

ALISON ROTHWELL

"I first met Nick James when I was a protégé student of his and I got the opportunity to work one-to-one with him and thoroughly enjoyed the whole thing. As a result, Nick helped me to grow my business to 6 figures from more or less a standing start."

BAL AND JEEVAN SINGH

"Hello Nick... I have learnt a great deal from you and your products and services. Over the years I have also been trickle feeding the principles you teach to my children.

My son Jeevan showed a particular interest.

Jeevan studied your materials meticulously and since then he has been engrossed in online marketing and information publishing.

To cut a long story short ... I just wanted to say "Thanks Mate" - All your advice & guidance paid off handsomely. Jeevan managed to get his book into the top 5 selling books in the UK and he is on his way to becoming a member of the 7 figure club."

ISAAC VELLA

And finally, here is another successful student of mine. Isaac is just 28 years old and was fed up to the teeth with his "day job" working as a car mechanic. So fed up, as it happens, that after being treated particularly badly by his boss one day, he decided to finally quit.

With just £80 in his pocket and funding his new business by selling his snap-on toolbox, together with its contents, for £800, Isaac not only had some seed money to start his new online business but also prevented himself from being tempted back to his old profession.

After receiving some initial training from me, Isaac pulled in over £40,000 GBP/$54,277 USD in sales from his Internet business in the first 8 months alone.

4

Why Information Publishing?

Now you've learned about the 5 Myths that are holding you back from being successful, you'll be able to identify them when they show up and make the right choices to keep you on track and heading toward your goal, without being distracted - or letting your mind be sabotaged subconsciously.

So let's move onto the third thing I promised to share with you... *Why Information Publishing?*

If I could spare you from anything, it would be to banish the thought that simply becoming self-employed or starting a new business will be the answer to your prayers. Unfortunately, many people think it is.

It's not.

People often risk their life savings to set themselves up with a traditional bricks-and-mortar business - and even go to the bank to re-mortgage their home - so they can invest in a franchise. They hope to create their fortune and live the American Dream, when in fact all they've done is simply replaced a thankless boss and a regular pay check with the "joy" of managing extreme business debt, cash-flow problems, and irate customers. And they're still exchanging hours for money. To top it all off, when you're self-employed you also have the pleasure of paying yourself *last*. Only when all your business expenses have been paid at the end of each month can you even begin to think about paying yourself some of what's left.

And I should know. Since leaving school I bought a window cleaning route, worked as a taxi driver and as a mobile DJ, and even tried operating a yard and garden maintenance business. All these businesses had the same problems.

In contrast, since meeting my "white knight" entrepreneur friend in the parking lot that cold and wet day back in 2001, I've gone on to sell thousands upon thousands of copies of "paper and ink" or information-based products, which people gladly pay me anywhere from $1–$9,997 to receive.

For example: You can create a 10-page special report in **two hours** or less. You can create all the marketing materials required to encourage customers to buy it in another hour.

Setting up a website or listing it for sale elsewhere online takes **half an hour max**. In just **three and a half hours** you can have a completely new information product ready to sell for $9.97 - it's not uncommon for me to sell *hundreds* of these.

But that's not the end of it. You can then invest a few more hours, recycle the content and convert this small report into a premium-priced product that will earn you $97 or more. You could also set up a membership site with 12 of these reports and get $20 monthly residual income for a year. You could sell licensing to a collection of your reports to other publishers for $297, and you could also offer some personal coaching via email or package and sell interaction with your customers as an e-class for $997.

The Information Publishing business is truly amazing: In the typical time (8 hours) someone else spends each day holding down a regular 9-to-5 job (again, swapping their time for money) and getting paid once to work, you could easily create an information product that pays you handsomely, over and over again, over the coming days, weeks, months, and even years to come.

We were on the way to a business meeting in Atlanta recently and I finished up a 19-page small report on "how to turn browsers on your website into buyers" on the flight there. **Another income stream.**

My mother-in-law lives about 60 minutes away, and on a couple of drives to and from her home to visit (*no, I wasn't driving*), I wrote a small report on "how to increase your sales copy conversion rates by making tiny changes." *Another income stream.*

These seemingly small sales can add up to quite significant amounts very quickly.

Using the two example reports I've just mentioned, even just ONE sale a day for each of these two reports would add up to $598.20 a month. That's just one month's income from two simple reports. Take out a calculator and see how quickly things can add up when you have a dozen or more information products for sale.

These information products are so easy to write that you'll find you can easily create them even in the shortest amounts of time.

That's what I love about the Information Publishing business- it doesn't take much time at all to create a dozen or so pages of information. In the typical time you'd spend a day at your regular job, you could create a small report using the system I use.

You don't *have* to limit yourself to "paper and ink" products, by the way. Or even write them yourself, if you don't want to.

I also have dabbled with offering simple software products, and I have hired low-cost ghost writers and licensed content in the past. However, I don't want you to get overwhelmed with too many choices at the outset. You *do* need to know how to pick a good product and what magic criteria to apply. Which I'll be revealing, all in due course.

Before we move on, however, let me qualify what I'm saying with this.

If you are already running a traditional business of your own and it is doing reasonably well for you, then hang onto it while you are looking into the benefits of an information publishing business.

For the moment, I want to concentrate on explaining in more detail why I think you should seriously consider concentrating your efforts on an Information Publishing business.

A 'Traditional Business'

First of all, let me tell you what it's like running a traditional business:

It's absolutely *crazy* - that's what it's like!

I've dipped my toe in the water several times with different businesses, so I know what I'm talking about. Running any kind of traditional business is a constant heartache. I'm not saying it's out of the question for you to do this. Many people make a modest success with them, and there's no reason why you shouldn't, either. It's just that there is a much, much *easier* way of making money than running a conventional business. By *traditional*, I mean a business that:

1. Has premises, no matter how small.
2. Employs people, no matter how few.

I state, here and now, that when you start out you should:

AVOID BOTH OF THESE HIDEOUS PRACTICES AT ALL COSTS!

Sound a bit crazy? Surely *all* businesses have premises and employ people, as a bare minimum?

These are the key features of a business, aren't they?

Not in *your* Information Publishing business, they're not!

Why?

Because this book and the whole idea of starting an Information Publishing business is ideal for *normal* people. People who haven't got $40,000+ to invest in even a tiny business (the average sandwich shop would cost you $100,000 to set up and fit out properly). This book is for people with no business experience whatsoever. People with only a few hundred dollars to start a business, and even that is hard to come by. People who know nothing at all about renting premises, hiring staff, borrowing money from banks, the IRS, taxes, liability insurance, health and safety at work, cash flow forecasts, accounting, fire regulations, toilets for the disabled, etc.

It's *easy* if you've got a spare quarter of a million and you're casting around for a good business to buy. It's *simple* if you've just spent four years on a business study course at your local college or university and know everything there is to know. Right? But where does that leave the *normal* person, the person who simply wants to improve his or her life, to get a better standard of living for the family, and to be freed from the treadmill of working for someone else?

Answer: They're screwed!

Business quickly becomes a closed shop, almost a secret club. Membership requires a lot of knowledge of business matters, **together with a serious amount of start-up cash** - and I'm talking about $40,000 <u>as an absolute minimum</u>. More likely much more. So most people give up, or don't even consider running their own business. But they haven't found this book!

Because there really *is* a way by which a hard-working, normal person of average intelligence and ability can start their own business and make a reasonable wage. I've proved it. I was in your position not so long ago.

It is, of course, the Nick James way! This is the way I will be revealing to you right here in this book, and, of course, **the business is Information Publishing.**

Now, over the years of being in this business, I have received hundreds of letters from people asking me what my "secret" to making money is. These letters have come from totally unconnected people around the world, and yet these people all had exactly the same desire! Uncanny, isn't it? And yet I'll be prepared to wager that *you* have these same desires, too.

Let me tell you what they all (and I mean *all*) wanted:

1. Loads and loads of money.

2. A legal, practical and ethical way of making this money.

3. A business that they could run part-time at first (evenings and weekends) until they proved the concept, and then move into full time. In other words, they didn't want to risk giving up a good job (if they had one) to move into a risky venture that could leave them stranded.

4. A business that required no staff and no premises.

5. A business that required almost no start-up capital (only because they didn't have any!).

6. A business they could run regardless of their age, sex, race or educational qualifications.

7. And, last but not least, a business that was *fun*, as well as being highly lucrative.

Sounds pretty good, eh? What's that? You wouldn't mind a slice of this action yourself? You see - **I was right all along!** The Information Publishing business offers exactly this - and then some! Let me tell you something:

I spend every minute of my working day operating this business. I will not touch *any* other business because *all* other businesses are feeble when compared with this business - as you already know, I've tried quite a few in my time. This is the only business worthy of my time, or your time for that matter, and this is the only business I recommend to people who happily pay $2,000 a shot for my one-to-one words of wisdom!

No other business will offer you the chance of making serious money, and certainly no other business can be operated so effortlessly from the very first day. What's more, this business can be run from your own home. There is no need to rent expensive premises or employ staff. You can run this business evenings or weekends, and you can *easily* make more money in one evening than you do in one month of your normal life. This is not an exaggeration. Information Publishing is a huge growth area, and if you get it right, **you can make millions and millions of dollars - just like me.**

But first things first. Consider this:

Information Publishing is the only business I know that offers **positive cash flow**. This means that the customers *pay first* and then *receive their goods later*. In almost all other businesses, you have to supply goods and services, and then *grow old* waiting around for people to pay you for what you've done! I know. I've been there too.

In the Information Publishing business, you wake up each morning to a stack of sales confirmation emails in your email inbox, all confirming money has been paid into your credit card merchant account or PayPal account. I've had so many emails some mornings I've been unable to see any other emails in my inbox without continuously scrolling the mouse down and down!

Like me, you too, could soon find yourself at the stage where you have to pay people just to count your sales and check your orders each day. Call me an old Scrooge, but I never get tired of counting money! It's a *great* way to start the day!

If that doesn't convince you, let me tell you that the Information Publishing business is the *cheapest* business I have ever heard about, in terms of start-up cash required to get going. **It costs less than one-tenth of the money required for even the cheapest traditional business.**

Why?

Because you have almost *no stock* and *no overheads*. You don't rent premises or pay business rates, or hire staff. Also, you need no working capital to cover the time it takes to get paid in a normal business.

Information Publishing is beautifully *testable*. This means that you create your product and marketing materials and try it out on a few hundred people to see if it works. If it does, then you just roll out thousands more (in your own time, of course), and make megabucks. If it doesn't work, then you try a different product or a different angle, again and again, until you get a winner.

With Information Publishing, you always start with either free or very small, cheap ads to see if the product idea looks good. Only then do you invest in larger and more expensive promotions.

Now this doesn't mean that any fool with a new information product and a one-page website can produce a winner immediately and hit a home run. In my experience, **it takes a lot more than that!** Of course it does. It stands to reason that you need something else to make it work; otherwise every reader of this book with $500 and a simple e-book would be out there clogging up the Internet and making a fortune!

So what do you need to succeed in this business?

You need a helping shove from an acknowledged expert in the field of Information Publishing, and that person is none other than shy, retiring, self-effacing, modest, little-old me!

Seriously, I've made a lot of money getting to know what does and doesn't work when it comes down to it! I've spent *years* learning the hard way, and I'm going to be passing on every detail to you so that you can emulate my success.

Believe me, it's a total jungle out there, and without someone to show you the way, you will almost certainly *lose money* at this. However, if you follow my advice, I promise that you will have absolutely the best chance of making some serious money (and remember, the goal here is at least $100,000 a year), with minimum risk.

I am prepared to teach you, if you are prepared to learn.

I'll happily tell you every little tip, every little strategy. I'll hold absolutely nothing back. After I've finished with you, if you can't make a steady income from Information Publishing, then there's no hope for you!

Heck, while I'm at it, I can think of quite a few more advantages of this business:

1. It's anonymous. Nobody needs to know who you are, if you don't want them to.

2. No one knows how much money you are making. You could make a million dollars on one ad (unlikely, by the way!), and no one would be the wiser. This stops competition dead in its tracks.

3. There is no face-to-face selling involved.

4. You never have to go cap in hand to the bank for money, as your cash-flow is *always* positive. In fact, you often find yourself with large amounts of money on deposit at the bank. I make thousands of dollars each year in interest, which the bank pays *me*, thanks to my overnight deposits of cash.

5. It's clean. It's not heavy work. You can do it in your own time - midnight till 5 in the morning, if those are the hours you keep.

6. There is no travelling. You don't even need a car!

7. You hardly ever see or speak to your customers (unless you want to).

8. There are no hidden costs. You know, in advance, exactly what everything will cost you, down to the last penny. This allows you to plan.

The benefits just go on and on and on. This really is the best business for the normal person to be in.

Every other business is a nightmare of rules, regulations, overhead and paperwork. Sure, if you feel that God has called you to start a steel-smelting plant, *then go ahead*. But the prime aim of starting any business is to have fun and make money, right? I mean, we're not out to save the world or anything! You want to work about *half as hard*, have fun, and *make at least four times a normal salary*, right? Don't lose sight of that! You want to do this in an *easy* way, okay? You don't want to be on some sort of giant ego-trip here.

The object is:

TO MAKE MONEY, TO HAVE FUN, TO TAKE IT A BIT EASIER

I sincerely hope that you're with me on this one!

Let's look at premises, for example.

When you are just starting out in business, you have this sort of vision of how it will be. The vision varies from person to person, but basically you see these really nice premises, with a new carpet on the floor, brand-new oak desks, leather swivel-chairs, maybe even a fountain in reception? You see yourself rolling into the car park in your new Mercedes, slipping into the space marked RESERVED, strolling through the swivel doors (perhaps with a polite, but not overly friendly "Morning, Hargreaves" to the doorman) and ascending the elevator to your penthouse complex.

Okay, perhaps that's a little over the top, but I bet you've thought of something along these lines, right? Come on, admit it, there's only you and me in the room!

Well, let me tell you that I've seen more companies go bust because the directors were on some giant ego trip than ever went belly-up through lack of business. Being your own boss *is* a bit of an ego trip, isn't it? Particularly for men (women are *far* more sensible). Men feel the point of the exercise is so that they can say: "Two cups of coffee please, Sandra," or "Hold all calls, Jeremy, I'm just heading to a board meeting." But let me tell you here and now:

This is all complete and utter BS!

You *must* restrain your plans for global domination if you are going to be successful in business.

People who know me often hear me joke that any company that has a fountain in reception is going to fail. Actually, you rarely see fountains in reception nowadays, but the principle stands. The point of the observation is that fuelling the egos of the company directors costs a *huge* amount of money. And you don't have huge amounts of money when you start out. In fact, you often have hardly any at all.

This is why I specifically liked a business that could be run from home (and you should, too).

You cannot get cheaper premises than your own home, as they are rent and tax-free because you're paying for them anyway. Even a shed somewhere will cost you a few hundred a month, and you really need this few hundred in your business, not pouring out of a sieve.

If you are prone to the premises ego trip, you won't like the idea of working from home; it's not classy enough, and you can't show off your new company to family and friends. But we're not talking about egos here, we're talking about starting a successful business that will grow and hopefully make you rich one day. The time for strutting around is later, when you've "made it." For now, help yourself to a giant serving of humble pie - that is, if you want to be eating caviar later!

The really beautiful thing about my business is that it can be started from a desk in a bedroom - *and this is exactly how you must start it* (on this scale, I mean), if you are to follow in my path. But many people think that they cannot work from their home. Here are the most common excuses I hear: *"My husband/wife wouldn't like it."*

If you are attached and your partner is not fully, 100% behind you in what you are trying to do, then you will not succeed anyway. The backing of your partner is absolutely essential if you are to make money with Information Publishing (or any other business). You can't fight the world *and* an unsympathetic partner. Presumably your partner is happy to share in the spoils of your success. Yes? Then he or she is going to have to put up with the inconveniences as well.

"What would the neighbours think?"

Who cares? I mean, you're not starting a steel-smelting plant in the back shed, are you? The Information Publishing business is completely low-key, so your neighbours almost certainly won't object. Anyway, if all goes well, you can think about taking a small office somewhere after a year or so.

"My suppliers and customers would not like coming to a private house."

First, most of your business will be conducted online, and even if a few suppliers did have to come to your home, this concern is still completely unjustified. I know from experience. I used to think that it would put people off, but it never did. You see, all those people slaving away for big companies, particularly the more senior people, have a secret desire to go it alone. They admire the small-scale operation, and they are quite prepared to support it - as long as the product or service is good of course.

There are also pitfalls to working from home:

The biggest problem is ensuring a separation of your *working* life from your *home* life - and this is vitally important. It doesn't matter if you work until midnight at the office; when you pack up and come home, then you're home. There is a clear distinction between the two. But when you run a business from your own home, if you don't get it exactly right, the edges will blur, and this can lead to problems. You'll find yourself working until 8 p.m., then watching a TV program, then going back to work for another two hours. Or worse, you'll bring work into the living area to do while you're watching TV, or talking, or whatever.

If you work from home, you must separate the two activities clearly and distinctly. The best way to do this is to have a spare room that's used only for the business. Failing this, then use half a room, or a desk in a room.

You should also have fairly strict rules about the time to stop working. It doesn't matter if you decide to stop at 10 p.m.; that's fine, just don't go back at 11 p.m. to finish a "quick letter."

This, without a doubt, is the biggest danger in working from home. *You're never away from it,* and the temptation to just open your laptop or "pop into the office" for another half-hour is almost overwhelming. Enormous self-discipline is required from you.

One final word on this, just in case you haven't got the message yet:

There is only one legal way of getting out of the 9-to-5 grind and swapping your hours for money, apart from luck. This way is to start your own Information Publishing business. It's fun, too.

Most traditional businesses are a first-class pain in the rear. They require lots of money at the beginning. They require your life's efforts for at least five years before the rewards start flowing to you. Most traditional businesses fail within two years of start-up, resulting in huge personal financial losses for the owners.

I say: *Forget all that.* I suggest starting a business that requires no premises, no staff, no overheads (to speak of), and most importantly - no large start-up capital.

Instead, follow what I share with you in this book and within the free download package that comes with this book (*Page vi*). I show you exactly how to start this business from scratch. When you start making a profit from your business, then you can reinvest a little at a time on improving the business - *but not before.* Then, and only then, when you've made a *lot* of money, I might just consider letting you rent an office and put a fountain in reception - if you really have to!

5

4 Key Components

Now you know why Info Publishing stacks the deck so heavily in your favour, let's move onto the *fourth thing* I promised to share with you: the *4 Key Components* vital for your business. You're going to love this. Copy what I show you and your business will grow like you can't imagine. The goal is to *add $100,000 per year* to your online information business, starting right now.

First, let me remind you that you are running a *business*, and that the business of every business is *to make money*!

The problem most people have is that they have an information *hobby*.

Let me show you what's possible. Imagine you have 2 products for sale on your website; one sells at $47 and the other for $297, and let's imagine you get 100 visitors a day to your site.

That's a total of 3,000 monthly visitors. At a 1% conversion rate of customers buying your first product, you'd make 30 sales a month at $47, for a total of $1,410. And with one in 3 of your new customers also buying your second product, that would add $2,970 more to your bank account.

So that's $4,380 in sales income per month, or $52,560 per year.

Sounds good, right?

But that's not everything. What if, of those buyers, 20% bought from you *every year,* and kept buying from you every year. It happens. My top 20 customers who bought from me online have continued to spend with me over the past 5 years. If you had 20 customers like those, you'd make ***$619,007*** over 5 years simply because 20 people had stumbled over one of your webpages.

Now imagine if you had customers like this that stayed with you for 10 years, or 20 years.

That's why you should be a *smart* entrepreneur, and treat what I'm sharing with you as a business, not a paid hobby.

Now, talking of *smart* entrepreneurs: When Walt Disney's girls were young, Saturdays were set aside to spend time with them. He would take them to various spots where the girls would play and enjoy themselves. As he watched them play, it occurred to him that he was on the outside looking in. He dreamed of a place where children and parents could play together. Disneyland became that place.

Walt Disney at the opening of Disneyland California in 1955

You see, what started out as a heart-warming expression of love for his own girls, and a desire to help other parents connect with their children, developed into a *multi-billion-dollar business.*

While making money may not have been the initial objective, it certainly turned into quite the money-maker!

Throughout the rest of this book, I'm going to show you how to turn your existing online business into "quite the money-maker" too.

Back to something I mentioned earlier: the damn surest way I know of, to make money selling information products, is to *AME.*

And as you know by now, that means to:

- Always add value
- Make a difference, and
- Enrich people's lives

In other words, the surest way I know of to make money is to always provide valuable content that enables other people to achieve their goals and reach their dreams.

Zig Ziglar: an immensely popular author, and motivational speaker.

Zig Ziglar, who was perhaps one of America's greatest authors, info marketers and motivational coaches in the self-help space, said it best:

"You will get all you want in life if you help enough people get what they want."

Walt Disney knew this secret as well. When he created a place where children and parents could enjoy spending time together, the money soon followed. And a lot of it.

I suggest Zig Ziglar's quote to you as a motto and a foundational cornerstone for your information business, as I have done for mine.

That's because, while following that principle results in getting what you want (financial gain), it originates with helping others get what *they* want.

Everything I'm about to share with you needs to be built upon this premise. When you do the 4 things I'm going to suggest, they should always be done with the intention of helping others get what they want.

When that happens, you will get all you want. Money will follow. A lot of it.

Psychologists call this the law of reciprocity. The Bible refers to it as "reaping what you sow." However you label it, the concept is the same: what you do for others not only benefits them, but returns as a benefit to yourself.

With every information product I create, I strive to create something that is loaded with benefit to the typical customer.

That's why I share so many details. And provide so many examples. And give so many tips. When you make your way through my information, I want you to feel good about me and my products. I know that the end result will be beneficial to us both.

Whether you sell to business people or parents or bodybuilders or educators or mechanics or whoever, do yourself a favor: help them get what they want. In doing so, you will automatically increase your business bottom line. That is, after all, the goal. Right?

With that foundation in mind, let's look at 4 Key Components of a *6-figures a year* strategy for your information business.

If you have not yet reached the 6-figures annual income level with your information business, then these 4 Key Components should serve as a good primer to illustrate what you need to do to reach this level.

If you're already generating beyond $100,000 a year, then doing these things can add a further $100,000 to your bottom line.

Actually, the potential is *much higher*, but I don't want to be too zealous.

And finally, if you're not yet selling information products online, then now is an ideal time to start. ☺

So let's take a look at each of these 4 Key Components.

Key Component 1: Increase Your Market Reach

Your *reach* is defined as your "range of effective action, power, or capacity."

Said another way, it is a measure of how far something is

outstretched. When I speak of market reach, what I mean is that you want to have your brand (and your products) permeate your market.

You want saturation. You want as many prospects to know about the product(s) you are selling as possible.

If I were going to create a formula for this measurement, it would look like this:

Website Traffic + Opt-In List Size = Market Reach

That is to say, how much reach you have in your specific market is measured by how many visitors you receive to your website and how many subscribers you have on your email list.

On sheer numbers alone, the larger your volume of traffic and the larger your list, the more money you will make.

EXAMPLE: *All things being equal, 10,000 website visitors will generate more profit for you than 1,000 website visitors. All things being equal, 25,000 opt-in subscribers will generate more profit for you than 5,000 opt-in subscribers.*

The important thing to remember is to direct more traffic to your website and secure more subscribers onto your list in order to convert them into paying customers for your various offers. The more *market reach* you have, the more sales you'll bring in just on the extra volume alone.

So, what's your plan for this?

How will you get more traffic to your website and get more subscribers on your list?

Really, it comes down to website traffic. You should have an opt-in list available at your website so visitors can join. So, it's really a matter of getting more people to your website so they can both join your list and buy your product.

How will you do this?

While there are dozens upon dozens of ways to generate free website traffic, let me save you some trouble by making a suggestion for you. I've been in this business for almost 17 years and 99% of my free website traffic comes from *one source.*

And yes - it's completely free.

So here's an important rule: Focus on getting "affiliate" traffic.

Let me answer 3 questions that I know you are probably asking right now.

Question 1. What is "affiliate" traffic?

Affiliate traffic is website visitors that other people generate for you. That is, other people (a.k.a. "JV partners") send their best prospects and customers to you, in exchange for a commission.

Other people already have high-traffic websites and large lists. Instead of you working like crazy to build your own business, you invite other people to send you what they already have in their possession.

Question 2. Why should I focus on affiliate traffic?

There are many reasons I believe affiliate traffic is the best, when used properly. First, it's completely free. Yes, you are paying a commission (usually 50%), but the traffic itself costs you nothing. And don't forget, *you* earn 50% yourself on every order generated through *other people's traffic*. Getting 50% of lots of traffic is much better than 100% of no traffic at all.

Secondly, it helps you avoid having to learn all the latest

strategies and buy all the latest software to do it yourself.

It eliminates all kinds of hurdles and challenges you might otherwise face, not to mention headaches as parameters and terms of service change and force people to do things differently.

You simply let other people learn the new stuff and send you traffic in the process!

Question 3: How do I get it?

The first thing you need is an affiliate program. People will send you traffic, but usually only if there is a financial benefit to them. There are many options, such as ClickBank, WarriorPlus and JVZoo, among others. Search Google.com for "set up an affiliate program" for details. If you use one of the previously mentioned services, setting things up is very easy, as they handle almost everything for you.

Once you have an affiliate program in place, there are lots of options for getting other people to promote your products for you. I'm going to share 4 of my favorite ways to get others to promote my products.

1. Guest blogging

Many bloggers allow "guest posts" on their blogs. That is, they allow outsiders to submit articles of varying lengths that they publish on their blog. At the conclusion of the post would be a brief reference to the author of the post, along with a link to their website. You could do nothing more than go on a guest blog tour (posting to new blogs regularly, week after week) and generate lots of traffic. If those reading the blog like what you've written, there is a good chance they will click through and visit your site.

2. Host a webinar

One of the more popular ways to generate traffic is through the use of webinars that you can promote using social media.

A webinar is simply an online presentation whereby participants at other locations can see and hear the presenter. You can create a webinar where you present 45 to 90 minutes of content from the comfort of your home, and have other affiliate partners promote it. In other words, your partners let people know about the webinar and invite them to register and join in to watch it.

During the presentation, you would then promote your product and attendees would visit your website for further details.

3. Affiliate contest

Perhaps my favorite way to get a quick boost of traffic (and consequently, orders) is to hold an affiliate contest. That is, for a specified period of time, you track sales for orders generated by affiliate partners. You award prizes for the top sales generators. You can also randomly choose participating affiliates, who might not have achieved top status, for additional prizes. Affiliates often scramble to promote these events because they receive their normal commission plus these added bonuses.

Another option is to create an incentive promotion. For example: Anyone who generates X number of sales during the next Y days get Z prize.

4. Interview

As the author of your product, you are also someone who can be the featured guest of an interview. Interview formats range from guest blog posts to podcasts to webinars to video presentations, and so forth. Perhaps even getting yourself heard on local or national radio.

The idea is simple: your partner promotes the interview to get a lot of people tuning in for it. They then ask you questions related to your area of expertise. During the interview - usually towards the conclusion - they pitch your product. Those listening/reading/watching the interview are then encouraged to visit your site and buy. Many will.

Now, can I suggest a bonus method?

If you don't want to set any of these things up yourself, another option for getting affiliate traffic is to find and work with a *joint venture broker* or an affiliate manager.

What this person does is set up guest blog tours, webinars, contests, interviews and other traffic-generation strategies. In exchange, they get a percentage of your revenue. I work with a wonderful affiliate manager and he does a fantastic job at getting "Nick James, The Internet Business Coach" out there in front of partners who send me traffic.

Obviously, this is just a list of ideas to get you thinking. You will need to learn how to do one or more of these things to put the idea to work for you, but I hope you get how powerful affiliate traffic can be. Any of these 4 ideas can generate all the free traffic you'll need.

You can choose one of these ways and allow it to be your only source of free traffic for the coming year, and you could still get a lot of it!

Before we move on, I want to emphasize something about each of these types of affiliate traffic. Do you see what they have in common?

- You are the expert
- You are the featured contributor
- You are the center of all the attention

That's what makes this so, so powerful and profitable. All

eyes are on you. It's your time to shine. Instead of competing with a bunch of others, you are singled out as someone of importance.

That will get you traffic.

Bottom line for this first Key Component is this: you want more prospects.

Key Component 2: Increasing Your Conversion Rate

It's one thing to get more traffic (or *any* traffic) to your website.

It's another thing to get that traffic to turn into **revenue**.

Or, said another way: it's not enough to get people to your website, you need to *get them to buy*.

You want prospects to turn into paying customers. And browsers to turn into buyers. That is, you need to increase your *conversion rate*.

Conversion rate is the relation of orders generated to the number of visitors to your website. It is usually described in terms of the percentage of visitors who make a purchase. If 2 out of every 100 visitors to a specific page at your website purchase the offer showcased, then you have a 2% conversion rate for the offer on that page.

Conversion rate is one of those things most people don't pay much attention to, when they should be paying *a lot* of attention.

Why? It's simple:

Raising your conversion rate means more profits from the exact same amount of traffic!

Think about it in terms of numbers:

Scenario A:

You sell a $47 product that converts at 2%.
You make $94 per 100 visitors.
(2 sales x $47 = $94)

Scenario B

You sell a $47 product that converts at 4%.
You make $188 per 100 visitors.
(4 sales x $47 = $188)

Same traffic = 2 additional sales per 100 visitors.

That may not sound like a big deal if you're getting only 2 additional sales, but it is a HUGE deal. Do you realize that you just **doubled your sales**?!

Instead of 2 orders per 100 visitors, you received 4 orders.

That's not *just* an increase of 2 points in your conversion rate, it's a massive *doubling of your orders*. Imagine what that looks like as you get not just 100 visitors, but *hundreds of thousands* of visitors. That little bump in conversion adds up to *a lot of money.*

Now, there are numerous ways to boost your conversion rate. Some people have conversion dialed in like a science. It's an art form. They test and track every little detail so that their conversion rate is maxed out, as high as it can be. There are comprehensive courses on the subject, with hundreds of pages. There are software programs and services and coaching available. We're not going to get into all that here.

However, there are 3 basic ways to boost your conversions that I'll mention briefly for you to research further on your own. Then, I'll give you a bit more information on my favorite one.

Conversion basically depends upon 3 things: who visits your website, what frame of mind they are in when they arrive at your website, and what they see when they get there.

Each of these 3 factors are, to a great degree, under your control.

1. Who is it that visits your website?

It's important to *generate better traffic*. The origin of your traffic is critical. The better the quality of your traffic, the more likely you are to convert your visitors to buyers.

Let me offer a few suggestions on improving your source of traffic:

Suggestion 1: Make sure it's targeted

If you are selling a product for bodybuilders, for example, you'd be better off advertising to the muscle and fitness crowd than you would to the knitting and crocheting crowd.

You may be able to convince a few knitters to visit your site, but they are infinitely less likely to buy from you than someone who has a pre-existing interest in the kind of product you sell. It is absolutely mandatory that your traffic be targeted.

Suggestion 2. Your targeted source of traffic should be qualified

While not mandatory, it is certainly preferable that your traffic also arrive qualified to purchase. If you are selling a product meant for *advanced* clientele, then your conversion will be higher if you screen out *beginners*. If you are selling a high-priced product, then your conversion will be higher if you screen out people who will have a limited or non-existent budget.

If you are selling a product for women only, conversion will be higher if you screen out men.

Who is your ideal customer? That's who you want to attract the most, if possible.

Suggestion 3. Your traffic can be referred

Personally, I consider this to be virtually mandatory. That is, if at all possible, you want prospects to arrive at your website having been recommended to you by someone else.

When someone endorses you, it instils customer confidence. If the person arriving at your website trusts the opinion of the referrer, then by proxy, they trust you and your product.

The more you can get other people to send you their targeted, qualified prospects, the better!

So, how do you get such traffic? The solution is simple: use the affiliate traffic suggestions I gave you a couple of pages back.

Affiliate traffic incorporates *all 3 suggestions* in addition to having the numerous advantages I mentioned earlier.

2. What frame of mind are your visitors in when they arrive at your website?

The "warmer" they are, the better. Restaurants make the most money when people are hungry, right? No hunger, to the guys at McDonald's, means that no cheeseburgers are being sold.

Said simply, you want those visitors to arrive at your website *hungry*. Already warmed up to your offer. Already interested. In fact, to some degree, anxious to actually buy it.

This happens most effectively when you (or an affiliate) "pre-sells" the prospect.

On this point, I'm going to share with you an excerpt from one of my courses, where I teach how to pre-sell customers, which reveals a method I've been using for many years.

A Short Excerpt From My 'Free To Fee' Home Study Course

To begin, I want to share with you what I consider to be the ultimate strategy for moving people from "free to fee." I've been teaching this for more than a decade, and the phrase that I coined has been referenced many, many times by others.

Let me give you the phrase, then an explanation, and then some examples.

The phrase: *"Useful, but incomplete"*

That is the kind of content that gets people to buy. It's far and away the best strategy I've seen in almost 17 years of selling information and teaching others to do the same.

Provide others with *useful, but incomplete* content.

Here's what that looks like:

Useful: Your information must be something of value to the reader in and of itself. It should communicate knowledge and experience that is helpful and advantageous to the reader. But also…

Incomplete: Your information must be lacking, in that they can better use the information you shared by making a purchase. The information you give can be further explained or enhanced or employed by buying something.

I'm going to give you some examples to help make this clear.

To keep it simple, I'll refer to article examples - that is, 500 to 800 word articles - that are useful, but incomplete, and ultimately promote a product.

Example 1

If I wanted to promote a list management service such as AWeber.com or GetResponse.com, how could I use an article to do this with the "useful, but incomplete" approach? By writing an article that explains how to profit from email subscriber lists.

My article could explain *7 Ways To Make Money On Autopilot.* In it, I would explain various strategies to make money by setting up automated emails to go out to subscribers.

Now, that's useful. But, what's incomplete? They would still need a list management service to do this. And I just happen to know of a *great service they can use.* ☺ So I point them toward that service.

Example 2

If I wanted to promote my **Premium Product Profit Formula** course at PremiumProductProfitFormula.com, how could I use this strategy?

By writing an article titled *Your Checklist For Creating $97 Products In 48 Hours Or Less.* In this article, I would share the exact steps that I teach in my course for creating those $97 products in 48 hours or less, with a paragraph explanation of each of them. So, that's *useful,* but what's *incomplete?*

I've told them what to do, but I haven't explained how to do it. Buying the product gets them a detailed explanation of each step, with all my shortcuts and secrets.

Example 3

If I wanted to promote *UnfairAdvantageCheatSheets.com*, how could I use this strategy? By writing an article that explains *How To Write An Order-Producing Sales Letter*. I could be extremely thorough in this article, really covering the subject matter well. That's *useful*, but what's *incomplete*?

It takes a lot of time and effort to write a good sales letter, so I could point to the Unfair Advantage Cheat Sheets in a variety of ways - ranging from the fill-in-the-blank sales letters included, the complete step-by-step copywriting course included, and the hundreds of fill-in-the-blank templates included. (Plus, I would mention that the sales letter part of Unfair Advantage Cheat Sheets is just ONE of the many other components included!)

What I want you to understand is **the strategy** and why it works so well. It provides something of value to the reader in and of itself. But it also always points to a resource that makes the valuable content even better.

This helps to…

- Build trust by showing you know what you're talking about in the content.
- Warms up the reader to a potential purchase of the recommended resource.
- Initiates the sales process that is continued seamlessly at your website.

When someone reads your article or report, watches your webinar, listens to your podcast, or takes in your content in any other form, they get some benefit from it. It's quality information. It has value to the reader. They find it helpful. It is *useful*!

But, it's also *incomplete*. It can be made even better by **a paid purchase** that will do one of 3 things:

Explain: If the free content provides an overview of a how-to process, or it provides a list of ways to do something, or it identifies WHAT to do, a purchase can provide a complete system - a detailed explanation - of the core concept(s) shared in the free content. What was shared in part can be shared in full.

Enhance: Maybe the paid purchase shows a better way to do something than the article, or shares a shortcut for doing it, or provides case studies for how other people are doing it, or has readymade research or a brainstorming session of ideas.

Maybe instead of one idea showcased in the article, the paid resource gives *27 more ideas*. The free content is enhanced through a purchase.

Employ: You could use the paid purchase to provide software or templates or a service or some other resource that actually does what is taught in the free content for the reader. Or, there could be a paid purchase that is *required* in order to apply the information shared in the content.

I just want to establish this core strategy that we are going to build upon. It is a fantastic concept that is very, very effective for getting people from "free to fee."

Useful. But. Incomplete.

Provide value in your free content and point toward a paid purchase that will make that free content even more valuable to the prospect.

Before moving on, let me make an observation that is worth pointing out. The excerpt I've just shared with you is a very basic way to *pre-sell*.

To some degree, I have now *warmed you up* to my **Free To Fee** course. At a minimum, I've raised your awareness of it.

Maybe you'll click through today and check it out. *Maybe you won't.*

But it's now in your mind, locked away somewhere for another day. The next time you hear about the product, it will be a bit more familiar to you. Enough exposures, and perhaps you'll even buy it. Who knows?

And that's just a simple way to use free content.

There are many more ways that are even more effective, but you'll have to buy the course to get all the information that my paying customers get. ☺ Do you see how this works?

3. What do your website visitors see when they get there?

Now you have traffic, and you have traffic that's arriving already "warmed up" to your offer.

Now what?

The final thing you can do to increase your conversion rate is to improve your offer.

Here are a few things for you to tweak and test to optimize performance and ultimately increase your conversion rates.

- Your headline, call to action, guarantee, and other parts of your sales letter.
- Graphics, design and layout, and other visual elements of your page.
- Factors like your price point, perceived value, and bonuses.
- Use (or lack thereof) of deadlines, limits and other aspects of creating urgency.
- Format, delivery, packaging, and other aspects of your product.

These are just a few things you can tweak to improve your conversion rate. As you improve your offer, you will improve your conversion rate. The two are permanently intertwined.

The bottom line for this second component is this:

You want more prospects who become paying customers.

Key Component 3: Increasing Repeat Purchases

An age-old marketing law says this:

It's much easier to sell MORE to existing customers than it is to find new customers to sell to.

Your information business stands to gain serious momentum when your existing customers spend money with you again and again. The principle is clear:

The more each customer spends with you this year, the fewer customers you'll need to add an extra $100,000 to your revenue

So, let's talk about some options for getting customers to spend more money with you. There are several, but I'll mention 2 of my favorites.

Option 1: Recurring income

Recurring income is ongoing compensation from a customer at a predetermined time interval. In other words, the customer pays you again and again, in regular instalments. These regular instalments can be weekly, monthly, quarterly, bi-annually, or annually.

There are many reasons that every information business should have at least one stream of recurring income. Let me suggest a few that directly benefit *you*.

- **Recurring income builds loyalty**. Your customers really buy in to you and your products. They become members of your inner circle. They look to you for information. You are the authority, instead of your competitor.

- **Recurring income is predictable revenue.** You can rely on the re-bills to bring in a steady income each month. This serves as a great foundation of security for your business.

- **Recurring income gives you many new selling opportunities.** That is, with delivery of whatever the customer is paying you for, you have a chance to highlight another offer of yours, either in the resource itself or as an attached advertisement.

- **Recurring income is easy to upsell.** That is, when someone purchases one of your existing products, you can simply point that customer toward your source of recurring income as an option for them to add to their order.

As I said, there are many reasons that recurring income is a benefit to your business. These are just a few.

Now, that probably brings up a question: What is recurring income? Again, there are many options for creating recurring income. Let me mention 3 to get you thinking.

Suggestion 1: A membership site

A typical membership site is an arrangement where members pay you ongoing fees (generally monthly) for ongoing content. That is, there is no end in sight. They keep paying you. You keep providing content. This is usually in a password-protected members' area on your website.

Suggestion 2: A Fixed-Term Membership Site

This is a short-term arrangement, usually lasting 4, 6, or 12 months. A series of content instalments (often reports or videos) are released to the customer, one component per week or month, for the fixed-term period. The customer pays weekly or monthly for the content that you provide. When the period is over, the customer has received all of your content in the series, and you have received all of his/her money for the series.

Suggestion 3: Miscellaneous Software As A Service Subscriptions

A variety of services can also bring in recurring income. Included are contact management (autoresponders, email lists), hosting, web-based tools like Adobe Creative, Customer CRM systems like Infusionsoft, and so forth. In fact, anything that customers regularly make payments to access and use would fall into this additional category.

However you categorize it, this is a great way to get the same customer to spend more money with you. They simply pay you in repeated instalments. It doesn't take a genius to see the financial benefit:

> Customer buys an e-book from you for $20
> or
> Customer joins a fixed-term membership site from you for
> $20 x 12 months
> $20 vs. $240

Same customer, more money spent.

So, that's one idea.

Here is the other.

Option 2: Funnel income

Another option for getting your customers to spend more money with you is to create a funnel that progressively leads the customer to more and more buying opportunities at varying price points.

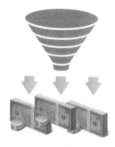

There are many things you could include in a funnel. I'm going to show you a typical funnel that I believe the average person can easily incorporate into his or her business from the very beginning.

While I know many people, myself included, have products and services ranging between $10,000 and $50,000, I won't include these here. These high-priced offerings are really a topic for another book.

Instead, I want you to get a realistic picture of what you can do with a funnel *starting immediately.*

Let's look at a typical funnel and then talk about how to facilitate sales between the various levels.

Level 1: ➤ $1 to $27 Simple report
Level 2: ➤ $40 to $97 Monthly membership
Level 3: ➤ $97 to $197 Premium product
Level 4: ➤ $297 to $497 Home study courses, etc.
Level 5: ➤ $497 to $997 Email coaching and big box products

So let's see what happens here. You do what we mentioned in components one and two: generate traffic and convert that traffic into a sale of a $7 report. The customer loves the report.

At the conclusion of the report - and in your follow-up email messages - they find out about your monthly membership site. They join it because they love your content.

Inside that membership site, one of the pieces of content they receive is an excerpted chapter from your $197 premium product.

They love the excerpt and want to read more, so they buy the full product.

At the beginning of the product, just after the title page, is an advertisement for your coaching. They'd love to work one-on-one with you, since they love your content. They buy the coaching.

Now, instead of getting $7 from the customer, you've earned well over $500 from that customer.

Not to mention, hopefully you've directly influenced that person's life in a positive way, helping them get what they want!

That's just one example of how to move the customer and facilitate sales from each level. (*By the way, there are other levels, such as licensing your content, but I'll save that for another day.*)

Here's the profound nature of this funnel: *Ultimately, you will have multiple offers at every level!*

That is to say, you might have dozens of $7 reports. You might have 3 or 4 (or more) membership sites.

You might have a handful of $197 offers (or two handfuls). You might even have multiple coaching classes.

And each of them points toward others, so you have amazing cross-promotion. If a customer buys anything from you, that customer is ultimately exposed to all of the available offers.

How? Let me offer just a few ideas.

Idea 1: In content references

That is, in the content for Product A, you can mention Product B. This can be as a case study (e.g., When I was researching X product, I found out...), or the introduction of an idea (e.g. One thing I teach in X product is...), or a suggestion (e.g. If you don't already have X, then I suggest you pick up a copy of X product), or any of a dozen other ways to mention your existing products in the content of another product.

Idea 2: Recommended resources

This one is super easy to do. At the beginning or ending (or both), you can reference all related products as recommended resources. In the beginning, you could have an About The Author page which has a list of your products with a 1-2 sentence description of each, along with a clickable link to their respective webpages. At the end, you can simply have a Recommended Reading section with a list of resources, a description of each, and a link to each.

Idea 3: Excerpts

This one is absolutely brilliant. Take 500–1,000 words from one product and use it as an excerpt in another product. Mention where the excerpt originated, provide a brief description of that original product, and then insert a clickable link for more information. Easiest cross-promotion you will ever find.

Idea 4: Free training creatives

When you create email mini-courses, articles, free reports, webinars, blog posts, or training pages like the one you are reading, then reference multiple products. Don't force pieces where they don't belong, and make sure your content-to-advertisement ratio is strong. But don't be afraid to use your free content to promote multiple products.

Idea 5: Upsell

> When you sell the $7 report, offer the $10 membership at the point of sale. I'll talk about that in the next section, but I wanted to mention it here to emphasize the idea of introducing the customer to multiple opportunities to make additional purchases.

When a customer spends more money with you, it moves you more quickly toward your goal of an extra $100,000 per year with information products.

I know we've looked in great detail at how to increase your revenue. And I've referred a lot to things like *getting more* from customers. Let me emphasize again, you get more from customers when you help *them* get more.

Don't lose sight of what makes this a win-win. That's easy to do when we're talking numbers. And I don't want it to sound like everything is all about making a buck.

The nature of this training is to teach you how to increase your revenue. This is *not* at the expense of the customer, but to their benefit.

You don't want to simply get their money; you want to provide them with information and resources that help them get what they want. In doing so, all of this training becomes easy to accomplish.

For example: Apple gets a lot of my money. But they do so because I get what I want from their products. Disney has gotten tens of thousands of dollars (and a lot of that is extra money through their marketing) from me, but I am not to be pitied, nor have I been exploited by them. They provided me with what I wanted for the money I spent. They didn't trick me or manipulate me or cheat me.

They convinced me to spend money on things I wanted. And they delivered. And that should be your business model too.

Key Component 4: Increasing Your Profit Per Transaction

Finally, you want the customer to spend *more* with each transaction. Not only are they buying more things, but they are spending more money on each of those things.

When I buy a television from the local electronics store, they don't just want me to spend $799 on a television. They want me to buy the $1,299 television. They also want me to buy an extended warranty plan. And a mounting bracket. And installation. And a cable subscription. And surround-sound.

When the transaction is finalized and I look at my receipt, they do not want me to see $799. They want me to see $1,799.

Same customer; more money spent per transaction.

Upselling this way is important because:

- As a customer, I'm "hot" when I say yes to making the initial purchase. I'm raising my hand and saying, "Yes!" I want to buy something. I'm prepared to buy something. I am, in fact, buying something.

- The store may never see me again. I might walk out the door and move to another town. Or make a friend who works at another electronics store. Or lose my job. Or become disinterested in television.

While you certainly don't want to overdo it (that can get so annoying: *Would you like this? Would you like that? Would you like a different this, and a different that!*), you want to take the opportunity to increase the transaction value, because that customer is ready to buy *now* and may never be ready to buy again.

Again, it's not junk you're pushing. And there is no need for tricks or pressure. Just give them the opportunity to spend more.

Let me share a quick story about how *not* to upsell...

Back in the mid-'00s, I went into a well-known electronics chain to buy a new Sony laptop for about $1,200. I go through laptops quickly (I purchase at least one new one each year), and so I declined the extended warranty.

The sales assistant told me it would cost about **$10,000** to replace the screen if it were to malfunction beyond the factory warranty (literally, that's what he said).

I declined again, telling him that I would likely buy another new laptop in less than a year, well within the factory warranty. He said, "Sir, you can't take that chance. Don't you understand, if you wait past the factory warranty and the screen malfunctions, you'll have to spend $10,000 to have it replaced!"

Uh, no, I'll be out $1,200 to buy a new laptop. Which is what I plan to do anyway.

Moral of the story: Don't be a moron in how you try to convince your customers to spend more money with you.

However, there are two very useful and effective ways to increase your profit per transaction that I want to mention:

Option 1: Point Of Sale Offers

One solid way to get your customers to spend more money with you is through an offer at the point of sale. These are usually in the form of an *upsell or cross sell.*

An *upsell* involves asking customers if they want more of the same, while a *cross sell* is asking if they want something that's related.

If you look to McDonald's, you'll see a perfect example of how this works.

> **Upsell:** "Would you like to supersize your order?" (More of the same)
>
> **Cross sell:** "Would you like an apple pie with that?" (Something related)

Here's a quick bonus tip: Make sure your cross sell really is related to your core offer, otherwise you'll have *moron* written all over your face!

To give you another example: A few years back, I was in a toy store with my son and we bought a couple of packs of baseball cards.

At the cash register the cashier asked, "Do you want batteries with that?" Hmm. Do these cards need batteries?

Remember what we've talked about: *Everything you do* needs to help your customers get what they want, not what you want to sell.

So only create your offers around this strategy, so you *both benefit.*

The idea is simply this: At the very moment a person is prepared to make a purchase, just present that customer with an *optional* additional item that could be purchased as part of the same transaction, which complements the original purchase.

The result? An almost instant guaranteed increase in your profit.

In my experience, anywhere from 10% to 50% of your customers will *automatically buy your upsell.*

(I once had an upsell that sold at a whopping 90% rate!)

Don't let what I said pass without reflection. There is a percentage - sometimes a hefty percentage - of your customers who will automatically buy the upsell just because you offer it.

That's right. Sometimes customers will *automatically buy*.

So, once you set it up, your profit per transaction will *automatically increase.*

***

Think about the numbers:

Sell 10 copies of a $47 product, you earn $470 for those 10 transactions.

Sell 10 copies of a $47 product and 3 units of a $20 upsell, you earn $530 for those 10 transactions.
(10 x $47= $470) + (3 x $20=$60) = $530

Instead of earning $47 per transaction, you earn $53 per transaction overall.

That's an extra $6 for every transaction.
This can be a huge amount of money over time.
A. Huge. Amount.

***

So, make sure you offer an upsell!

It could be:

- A special report
- A related product
- A bunch of articles
- Coaching
- Done-for-you service
- A membership site
- Trial offer
- Templates
- Other formats (audio/video)

And there are an unlimited number of other ways to do this. So let your imagination run wild!

Option 2: Premium Products

Most people will *not* succeed with a Walmart®-style business plan. That is, the average person - that's me and you - simply can't find the volume of customers required to make the low-cost offers model work.

In other words, *most people* won't make a significant amount of money online trying to make a small profit from a large number of people.

Consider this: If you're selling an information product that yields a $10 profit, you'd have to find 1,000 new customers per month to make $10,000 per month.

This is almost impossible to pull off even *once*, for most people. And certainly, rarely done month after month after month.

Low-cost information products simply aren't the answer for a significant, sustainable income. At least, not on their own.   ☺

The key here is, *not on their own*.

To be sure, you should have low-cost *entry-level* products. In fact, they are an integral part of any overall business plan, as I showed you earlier in the *funnel* section.

Instead, you want to sell products at a premium price: $97, $297, $497, $997, and more.

1,000 orders at $10 = $10,000
100 orders at $100 = $10,000
10 orders at $1,000 = $10,000

Trust me when I tell you that it is far easier to find *10 people* to spend $1,000, than it is to generate *1,000 orders* for a $10 product.

Far, far, easier.

The problem is usually having the ability to create a product that customers will consider is worth $1,000, right?

That's why I love to camp out around the $100 to $497 mark. More often than not, this has been a $97 product offering that sold in excess of 100 copies at that price point. This is extremely doable, and it is still far easier than selling 1,000 at the $10 price point.

One of my courses (www.SimpleProductProfitFormula.com) has actually sold over 1,000 copies at the $97 price point.

As an aside: I love this price point so much and have done so well with it that I have actually created a feature-length training on the subject of how to create your own $97 products in 48 hours or less at www.PremiumProductProfitFormula.com.

So, what can you do to create a $97 offer?

Let me give you 3 quick ideas, from **The Premium Product Profit Formula** Home Study Course.

Idea 1: Offer specialized training

Generally speaking, the more specialized the content, the more it costs. For example: a page from a recipe book won't command as much money as a page containing the combination to a bank vault full of gold bars. ☺

Seriously though, all content is not created equal. *Marketing 101* will generally not command as high a price tag as *Marketing 101 for Chiropractors*.

One easy way to increase your price is to specialize your content. Drill down at least 3 levels in your market. Here is an example from my own market.

Internet Marketing ➤ Product Creation ➤ Digital Products ➤ $97 to $197 Products

That's what I did for creating **The Premium Product Profit Formula.**

Idea 2: Personalized training

Personal coaching can be something as simple as email coaching, where you answer a customer's questions via email. Or a telephone consultation. Or video conferencing. Or live chat via Facebook. The idea is simple: the customer pays extra because they get to interact with you one-on-one to answer their questions and give them feedback. See www.iCoachingProgram.com for an example of how I offer this kind of coaching myself.

Idea 3: Optimized training

This is another one that I teach in **The Premium Product Profit Formula**. The idea is to create a PowerPoint© slideshow video training and add in valuable accessories like commentary reports, checklists, templates, swipe files, etc., to create a $97 to $197 package.

This is *especially* effective when combined with specialized information, as I mentioned earlier. Don't deliver your content as just an e-book or even a Kindle e-book. Instead, properly create and package it, and you can command a premium price for it.

And that's it for the 4 Key Components you need to know **to add an extra $100,000 per year to your information product business!**

These will:

- Increase your market reach
- Increase your conversion rate
- Increase your repeat purchases
- Increase your profit per transaction

6

Final thoughts and further reading

At the start of this book I said I would share with you 4 things. First, **my story** of how I went from mess to success. Second, the **5 myths** you've been led to believe by others that are preventing you from making $100,000 or more per year with your information business. Third, why the Information Publishing business is simply the best business model in the world for the normal person. And fourth, the **4 Key Components** that will help you add $100,000 per year to your online Information Publishing business, starting right now.

Let me ask you: Have you learned *at least* one new thing you didn't know before you read this book? Or were you at least reminded of something that you used to do?

While I've given you a *lot* of information and a ton of examples and options, you probably now want **a workable plan**, right? That is, you want something *concrete* to do with each of these key components to get everything in place. One simple solution for each part, if you will.

So, let me share this with you.

I have put the finishing touches on a brand-new, digitally delivered home study course that offers additional in-depth training, called **Six Figures A Year, _Starting Right Now_**. And I'm excited to share it with you.

This is going to make **a huge difference in your life**. Especially if you have enjoyed reading the thoughts, ideas and techniques I've introduced to you in this book and now you're hungry to know more. This is because this new home study course will take you by the hand and explain how to implement each of the 4 Key Components you've been learning about into your own Information Publishing business - no matter what type of information product you decide to create.

And remember, using all of these components is the key to your success and generating $100,000 a year from your Information Publishing business:

1.   Increasing your market reach
2.   Boosting your sales conversion rates
3.   Getting more repeat purchases
4.   Making more money per transaction

Now, I can't _promise_ that you'll make six figures a year. Heck, I can't even promise you'll make any additional cash, because I don't know you and I don't know if you're going to take any action whatsoever.

But what I can promise is that I won't hold anything back - I'll show you _the exact strategies_ I use to implement each of these four components into my business. You'll also find out how I personally make much more than just six figures a year myself.

So what you're going to get are my insider tips, tricks, and training. I'll give you plenty of samples and templates. And you'll get this training in a variety of formats - including audio, video and text (.pdf) - so you can learn the information in a way that works best for you.

For each of the four components you'll get one extremely detailed strategy for boosting your income. I've chosen strategies that are *easy to implement* and tend to produce good, reliable results.

When you decide to enrol today, you'll get access to *one session per month*. Simply put these four proven revenue-boosting strategies in place in the order I give them to you, and in four months you're going to have a rock-solid, revenue-producing Information Publishing business, set up correctly, that will help you go far and go fast.

So take a look at what you're going to discover in each month's training session.

Month 1: Price Points

How to increase your profit per transaction

One way to make more money in your business is to increase the amount of money every customer spends with you on each transaction. That means doing cross-sells and upsells to increase the order price. This session will show you how to do that. Plus, you'll also discover:

- The #1 easiest way to quickly boost the amount of each order - this is so simple that many marketers overlook it!
- Two profitable ways to offer an upsell. *(Many people only know one.)*
- Three types of upsells to offer - pick the one most profitable for you.
- How to turn an hour of your time into $200 - and do it over and over again!
- The secrets of offering a high-priced coaching upsell - without lifting a finger yourself!
- What a "toolkit upsell" is - and why your prospects will go crazy for it!
- How to create an upsell offer that works like gangbusters to increase profits - you'll even get a real-life example you can use as a model for your own offer.

Month 2: Purchases

How to increase your number of repeat purchases

In this exciting session you'll find out how to turn one-time buyers into rabid customers who purchase products from you again and again. Think about it - this is how you turn a $7 customer into a customer worth hundreds, if not thousands, of dollars to you!

Take a look at what you'll learn:

- The #1 way to get repeat purchases - just set it, forget it, and then watch the payments roll in on their own!
- What an FTM site is, and how you can use it to create a residual stream of income for yourself.
- A meaty, step-by-step guide for setting up your own profitable residual income stream.
- You'll discover the surprisingly simple tweak that transforms a regular membership site into a crazy ATM!
- A simple way to increase the perceived value of any membership site - it's so easy, but it gives an average membership site a premium feel!
- You'll discover the secret that's the real motherload of repeat purchases - once you know this strategy, you'll be able to snap a significant income generator into place!
- You'll even get 10 sure-fire tactics for getting your customers to buy from you again and again. This is where the money's at!

Month 3: Payments

How to increase your conversion rate

Here's how to give yourself an instant pay raise: you simply convince more of your existing visitors to buy your products or services. This simple tweak can add tens of thousands of dollars to your yearly revenue.

Here's what you get inside this eye-opening session:

- How to presell your prospects and turn them into hot leads using free content.
- A clever way to overcome your prospects' "defensive mind" and gently ease them into a trusting, buying mood.
- Why a "guide" works better than a report for bringing more cash-in-hand customers to your order form (this might surprise you).
- You'll get the complete step-by-step G.U.I.D.E. system for creating your own order-pulling guide.
- The "secret sauce" that gets people ordering like crazy from your guide - most marketers get this wrong and then wonder why their sales are flatlining!
- You'll discover the #1 thing people want from your guide. *(Hint: if you deliver it, you're going to have a whole bunch of new orders and customers!)*
- Five tips for writing your guide in a way that hooks readers and gets them hustling to your order form!
- You'll find out what separates an unread, mediocre guide from an attention-getting, order-pulling sales tool!
- Plus, you'll get 10 rock-solid, proven ways to get your guide in front of more people - and that means you'll get more of those sweet payment notifications rolling into your inbox!

Month 4: Prospects

How to increase your market reach

The fourth way to make more money with your information business is to get your offers in front of more people. And that's exactly what you'll learn how to do in this final session.

Take a look at these tips, tricks and strategies for getting more visitors to your sales pages:

- You'll find out how to put the C.E.N.T.E.R. System to work for you to get huge traffic gains!
- A simple "tour" strategy you can use to bring in a large

amount of traffic and bank a considerable amount of cash - it's easier than you think!

- How to set up a cash-pulling interview today (yes, *today*) using the "closed interview" model.
- The secrets of finding people with big audiences and persuading them to let you pitch to their audiences - this is a great (and totally legit) way to leverage other peoples' assets for your benefit!
- You'll get a list of 20 standard interview questions you can swipe and use to create your own profitable guest interview - it couldn't be easier!
- The #1 way to get prospects super-interested in your offer and champing at the bit to buy!
- Plus four other secrets for using free content to whip your audience into a buying frenzy so you can make more sales!
- How to quickly and easily turn your existing content into cash-pulling freebies. *(Hint: it takes just a few minutes, but you get a huge payoff!)*

As you can see, there's a lot of information jam-packed into these four monthly sessions. But it's all laid out in an easy-to-follow format so you can start implementing these techniques right away.

What's more, each month's training session includes:

1. Approximately 45 minutes of video training

Each of the four monthly instalments includes a video training presentation about 45 minutes long. This is a downloadable video you can watch on your computer any time; no need to be connected to the Internet or watch from inside a members' area. The video is yours to view any time, anywhere.

2. Alternative formats

You will also receive a word-by-word transcript of the training presentation delivered in .pdf format. You can read it on your computer, tablet, or phone. Or print it out to highlight and take notes. Also included is an .mp3 audio version of the training, in case you want to listen to it on your mp3 player while exercising or in your vehicle while commuting.

3. Customized accessories

Each month will also include an "extra" to enhance the training or give you a different option for completion. You will find these are actually as valuable as the main training itself - in some cases *more* valuable! I am widely known for over-delivering, so you know these will be good. And I am also known for these accessories being relevant and not just thrown in to raise perceived value.

The training itself is in my typical style - which is to say, it's damn good. Seriously, if you have purchased any of my products in the past, then you'll see this training is typical of what I do.

Here is what you can expect in these training sessions:

Lots of ideas and examples. One thing I really like to do is share examples so you really *get it.* Examples bring clarity to training. They let you know what the information looks like in real life. You'll find a lot of these in each training session. Plus an abundance of ideas - thoughts, variations, tweaks, options and so forth - to really put the training to work for you.

On-target strategies. Each of these training sessions ties directly into the four components of earning an extra $100,000 with information products. These aren't "also do this" ideas, but rather core strategies that are at the heart of how to make more revenue.

A proven, workable plan. I've chosen a path for you. I've narrowed things down for you. Nothing for you to pick from, just universal strategies that work for every information products business. One path. One way.

You don't need to figure out the moving parts; I've done this for you.

This is stuff you can put into practice immediately! But, there's one catch - this training isn't for everyone.

Are You Qualified And Eligible To Start The Training?

The Six Figures A Year training program is *not* recommended for everyone. In some cases, I'll explain the how-to process in step-by-step format. But in others, there will be "what to do" information that refers back to the contents of the Simple Product Profit Formula. *(See the recommended resources page of this book.)*

You see, if you're already selling information products, then this course will be like a catapult to take you to a whole new level.

Sounds fantastic, right? There's no question that **The Six Figures A Year training program** will be extremely helpful to anyone serious about starting and profiting from an Information Publishing business.

By now, your only question may be: *How much is this going to cost?*

My normal pricing for one-hour video consultations is $1,297. That's not a made-up figure; it's actually what I charge for an hour of my time (subject to availability), where I sit with you using Skype or Zoom or similar and consult with VIP clients one-to-one. You can check it out at my website to verify if you wish.

So, for a 45-minute session, my regular price would be $972 for each training session - $3,890 for **an entire four-month training**. That's a small price to pay for this sort of high-level training that gives you a proven six-figure strategy.

Think about it...

If every month's strategy brings you just *one* customer who's worth $972 to you, then you've recouped your investment. Every customer and every dollar you make after that is pure gravy. Pure profit.

And based on my experience, clients who put these strategies into play get many more than just four new customers - know what I mean?

Even though this training is worth every penny (and then some) at the regular price, because you invested in this book I am going to make you a very special offer: If you act now, you can grab this training for just **$47 per month** (for four months).

And that is an extremely sweet deal, considering the regular investment price to work with me one-to-one like this for *four whole months* would ordinarily be $3,890. *Right?*

So here's the deal.

This special **$47/month** pricing offer for this extremely powerful **4-month online course** won't last long, so simply visit the private special-offer link below to get *instant access* to your first monthly training right away.

http://www.SixFiguresAYear.com/specialoffer

I highly recommend you take this next step in your exciting entrepreneurial journey today.

You can do so safe in the knowledge that, once you're enrolled into the program, we will *automatically* let you know by email just as soon as your next month's training materials have been specially prepared and published for you in your private members' area.

Finally, I sincerely hope that you have enjoyed reading *Six Figures A Year In Information Publishing* and you have taken something positive and worthwhile from it.

Of course, how you take things forward from here is entirely up to you. As I write these last few words of the book, I am having flashbacks to the restless night I spent after watching the three video tapes I was handed in the parking lot that day in 2001.

I knew then I had stumbled onto something special. If you're feeling that flutter of excitement inside about what the future holds for you right now, that's a good thing. That's the feeling that will help you put everything you've just discovered into action.

I wish you the very best with your new and exciting Information Publishing business, and I look forward to hearing about your $100,000-a-year success soon.

With this in mind, to help get your new Info Publishing business off to a flying start, on the next few pages you have a list of *27 Red Hot Ideas* which should get your creative juices flowing for your next (or first) Information Product.

Appendix

27 Red-Hot Ideas For Your Next (Or First) Information Product

There are so many kinds of information products you can write, and when you mix-and-match them with different topics, you can create dozens upon dozens of highly desirable resources to sell online.

This appendix is actually one of my own previous special reports that I have repurposed and included in this book for you, so together we can examine a total of 27 different kinds of information products (along with examples) you can create. Use this list to brainstorm ideas for your next small report (and all those to follow!)...

1. How-To Tutorial

Our index begins with the classic "how-to" tutorial. This style of report is organized as a systematic, step-by-step approach to accomplishing a task. The steps are most commonly organized in chronological order (Step 1 is..., Step 2 is..., etc.). These are generally known as "systems," "formulas," "checklists," or "blueprints".

A few examples include:

1. *How to Design a Web Page in 5 Easy Steps*
2. *How to Lose 10 Pounds in 10 Days*
3. *How to Meet The Woman Of Your Dreams*
4. *How to Make Your First $1,000 Online*
5. *How to Teach A Sunday School Class*
6. *How to Make a Small Fortune Online With Small Reports*

2. Frequently Asked Questions

In this model you would collect 10 to 20 of the most-asked questions about a particular topic and answer them in your content. This is one of the easiest kinds of small reports to create, because outlining is simple thanks to the Q&A style:

1. *List the question.*
2. *Answer it.*

While you'll want to create a better title than the ones below, here are just a few ideas for how this kind of small report might be created.

1. *Top 20 Questions About Home-schooling*
2. *Top 20 Questions About Generating Site Traffic*
3. *Top 20 Questions About Saving A Marriage*
4. *Top 20 Questions About Adopting A Child*
5. *Top 20 Questions About Starting A Membership Site*
6. *Top 20 Questions About Self-Publishing*

3. Interview

Moving from questions that *you* answer to questions that *someone else* answers is another way to write a small report. An "*interview*" small report is, not surprisingly, a series of questions you pose to one or more qualified experts to create the content you'll be selling.

(Reasons why experts would do this for you include free publicity for their website or business, rights to the completed report, or paid compensation.)

Again, these aren't titles for your small report but some suggestions for what you might do for a handful of different topics:

1. *Ask a fitness trainer questions about weight loss*
2. *Ask a charity chairman questions about fundraising*
3. *Ask a travel agent questions about discount travel.*
4. *Ask a loan officer questions about securing a mortgage*
5. *Ask a real estate broker questions about selling/buying a home.*

4. List

Another popular kind of information product is the "list": a listing of ways, strategies, tips, secrets, tactics, techniques, habits, exercises, principles, etc., with a detailed description of each entry to the list.

Some examples of this kind of information product include:

1. *7 Ways To Automatically Burn More Calories*
2. *5 Little Known Weight Loss Strategies*
3. *50 Email Marketing Best Practices*
4. *The 3 "Advantages" You Need To Beat Your Tennis Rivals*
5. *Top 10 Time Management Tips You've NEVER Been Told*

5. Case Study

Next on our list of small report types is the "case study" model, in which you profile successful examples of how a common task was accomplished. In other words, you'd show how several people (including or not including yourself) have achieved the desired result.

The great thing about this kind of information product is the variety of different methods people use to attain similar results. Your readers will likely connect with one or more of the examples and get a sense of motivation and empowerment to reach their goal as well. Bottom line: you've got a satisfied customer.

A few examples include (these are ideas, not titles):

1. *Learn How 7 Stay-At-Home Moms Each Lost 20 Pounds*
2. *The Machine Weight Workouts of 7 Top Fitness Trainers*
3. *Outreach Program Plans of the 10 Fastest Growing Churches*
4. *10 Affiliate Marketing Campaigns You Can Legally "Steal" And Use to Promote Any Program You Want*

6. Resource Directory

The next kind of information product is the "resource directory": a list of resources related to a particular topic (usually indexed by category and then alphabetically), along with contact information, such as website, phone number and/or mailing address or geographical address.

Note: Several years ago, when public wi-fi access was almost nonexistent, I wanted to travel more - which meant taking my business on the road. I purchased one of these "resource style" reports online, which highlighted resources for connecting to the Internet, including a listing of places that offered wi-fi access. I paid around 30 bucks for the short report ... and loved it.

A few examples of this kind of small report would include:

1. *The New England Bed And Breakfast Guide*
2. *The Wholesaler's Resource Guide for Import*
3. *The Christian Publisher's Resource Guide*
4. *The Product Duplication and Fulfillment Source Book*
5. *The 101 Most Fun "Kid Friendly" Websites*
6. *The Top 50 Recommended Home-Schooling Resources*

7. Idea Generators

The "*idea generators*" style of information product is best described as "*a series of prompts to help the reader brainstorm ideas.*"

Here are a few examples:

1. *101 Idea Prompts for Fiction Writers*
2. *75 Starter Questions for Small Group Discussion*
3. *97 Winning Ad Headlines For Your Sales Letter Swipe File*
4. *101 Best Prayer Starters For New Christians*
5. *101 Fill-In-The-Blank Internet Auction Templates*
6. *The Ultimate Book of Ideas for Home-Schoolers*

8. The First Year

Up next is what I've labeled "the first year." In this kind of information product, you'd walk a newcomer through the first 12 months of a particular endeavor. What beginner standing on the threshold of something completely new to them wouldn't want the wisdom of what to expect and how to successfully navigate through the foundation period?

You could chronicle the first year, with a calendar of milestones and guideposts, pitfalls to avoid, shortcuts to take and so forth.

Some examples:

1. *The First Year of Parenting*
2. *The First Year of Home-schooling*
3. *The First Year of College*
4. *The First Year of Internet Business*
5. *The First Year of Life After Loss of Loved One*
6. *The First Year of Teaching*
7. *The First Year of Youth Ministry*
8. *The First Year of Living With M.S.*

9. Niche Business

One of the biggest mistakes most Internet marketers make is trying to create information products to sell to other Internet marketers. It's a cycle that just loops over and over again. Fortunately for you, while everyone else is competing with each other, you have an opportunity to teach "niches" how to market. Instead of selling marketing information to other marketers, teach niche business owners how to market. *All* business owners, regardless of what their business is, need more customers.

Note: What's interesting about this kind of small report is that you can make a few changes and "niche it" for numerous topics, i.e., "Bookstore Owner's Guide to Marketing," "Real Estate Agent's Guide to Marketing," "Hair Salon Owner's Guide to Marketing," etc.

Some examples:

1. *The Christian Bookstore Owner's Guide To Marketing*
2. *The Pet Store Owner's Guide To Marketing*
3. *The Personal Trainer's Guide To Getting More Clients*
4. *How To Quickly And Easily Get More Real Estate Referrals*
5. *A Crash Course In Free Publicity For Independent Singers*
6. *A 10-Day Plan For Promoting Your Craft Show*

10. The Bridge

I've labeled this kind of small report "the bridge," because the idea is to combine two unrelated topics into one information product. Think of it this way: there are universal wants and needs (e.g., to lose weight and get in shape) that are applicable to virtually *all* markets. Most people want to make more money, be successful, live happily, have great relationships, etc. These are universal pursuits. The idea here is to bring those universal pursuits into the arena of your specific field of interest or expertise.

Some examples:

1.   *Time Management For Single Parents*
2.   *The Internet Marketer's Diet*
3.   *How To Make Money Selling Baseball Cards on eBay®*
4.   *The Educator's Guide to Becoming A High-Paid Public Speaker*
5.   *Success Secrets For Small Business Owners*
6.   *The Home-Schoolers Guide To Working At Home*

11. Shortcuts

Who among us wouldn't like to take shortcuts (assuming there are no drawbacks) to achieve a desired result faster, easier or better? The short answer is: no one. With this kind of information product you would focus on ways to save time or effort in accomplishing a specific task without sacrificing any benefits or quality.

Some examples:

1.   *17 Money-Saving Shortcuts For Buying A New Home*
2.   *10 Shortcuts To Mastering Your Golf Game*
3.   *Top 10 Shortcuts For Using Adobe® Photoshop®*
4.   *5 Simple Shortcuts For Acing The SAT*
5.   *7 Shortcuts For Planning The Perfect Wedding*
6.   *Shortcuts For Writers: How To Write Faster, Easier and Better*

12. Advanced Guide

To an extent we've already talked about focusing your information product on "beginners." (See "The First Year" above.) But what about those who have an elevated state of experience or knowledge? There is a huge market for "advanced" information in just about every field. In the information age, this is especially the case, as more and more people have access to basic steps (usually rehashed, restated and repackaged in a thousand different ways!), creating a sort of traffic jam, with little higher learning available in many areas.

So, creating an information product focused on providing information for the experienced or advanced user is another great idea.

Note: To create a great one-two punch, why not write a "beginners" report on a topic and then create an "advanced" report on the same topic. Then you are able to "graduate" your beginners to the advanced report after they've read the first one.

Some examples:

1. *A Field Guide To Advanced Bird Watching*
2. *The Advanced Guide To Playing Poker*
3. *Advanced Affiliate Marketing Strategies*
4. *Tennis Drills For The Advanced Player*
5. *7 Advanced Selling Strategies For The Car Industry*
6. *Advanced Madden 07® Strategies: How To Beat Anyone, Anywhere, Anytime!*

13. Time Frame

With this kind of information product you would focus your positioning on the *time frame* in which the task can be completed. Everything would be structured toward seeing results within a specific period of time; that would be the selling point. More important than getting results is knowing how long it's going to take to get those results (assuming it's not long! ☺).

Case Study: Jim Edwards did this when he created a course titled "How To Write An eBook In 7 Days". It was a huge smash hit. There were numerous courses available at the time that taught how to write e-books, but his was the first that emphasized a specific time frame. The point: You can sell the same topic to a crowded marketplace if you stress a time period!

Some examples:

1. *How To Make Money Online In 10 Days Or Less*
2. *The 7-Day Weight Loss Plan*
3. *Rapid Restoration: Save Your Marriage In The Next 24 Hours*
4. *The Ultimate Guide To Writing Your Book in 30 Days*
5. *21 Days To Breaking Any Habit, Addiction or Weakness*
6. *How To Sell Your House In 2 Weeks Or Less*

14. Personal Profile

What's more likely to get your attention: an overweight friend who says "I've got some great information on losing weight," or a thin friend who used to be overweight who says, "Let me show you how I lost the weight"? Obviously, unless you're suffering from delirium, the thin friend gets your vote. Why? Because when we see that someone has achieved the results we'd like to achieve, there is credibility.

By creating an information product that reveals and explains how you accomplished a specific task that others want to accomplish, you should have an instant hit on your hands. In this kind of small report, simply chronicle what you did.

Some examples:

1. *How I Lost 20 Pounds Without Pills, Potions and Plans*
2. *How I Made $26,234 In One Week As An Unknown Marketer*
3. *How I Shaved 10 Strokes Off My Golf Score...And You Can Too!*
4. *How I Got My First Book Published And Into Bookstores Everywhere*
5. *How I Raised $1,000,000 For Our Local Charity*
6. *How I Beat Cancer Naturally And Safely*

15. Planner

Some of my most popular information products ever have been *"planners."* For our purposes, a "planner" is simply a set of activities arranged in a daily schedule as a sort of checklist to work through. Why do people love them? Because it allows them to *stay on track*. They see a set of action steps to complete for Monday, then Tuesday, then Wednesday, and so forth. Most people find it much easier to actually do something when it's arranged in this kind of order.

Note: This is one of my top recommendations for a small report. Every small report author should write at least one of these "planners" to sell online.

Some examples:

1. *The 7-Day Checklist For Writing A Small Report*
2. *The 31-Day Guide To Powerful Prayer*
3. *The Navy Seal's 7-Day Abs Workout*
4. *The 4-Week Wedding Planner And Organizer*
5. *The Smart Home-Schooler's Daily Schedule*
6. *33 Days To Internet Marketing Success*

16. What To Do When

This is a classic example of the "problem/solution" format. It's just expressed in a different way. The idea here is to inform readers what they should do when they find themselves facing a specific problem that can still be remedied.

A key is to focus on as specific information as possible in your title.

It's not, for example, *"What To Do When You Want To Lose Weight"* but rather *"What To Do When You Want To Lose That Last 5 Pounds"*.

Some examples:

1. *What To Do When You Need To Lose That Last 5 Pounds*
2. *What To Do When You're Raising A Strong-Willed Child*
3. *What To Do When Your Spouse Wants A Divorce*

4. *What To Do When You Worry Too Much*
5. *What To Do When Someone You Love Is Battling Addiction*
6. *What To Do When You Can't Get Pregnant*

17. Pop Culture Lessons

This kind of information product is for the creative writer. If you're not creative, then feel free to move on to #18.☺ The idea here is to share lessons that you've gleaned from pop culture (movies, music, lifestyles, fashion, entertainment, cooking, etc.).

One reason this is usually a very good seller is because of its inherent ability to create curiosity.

What email marketer wouldn't want to know Santa Claus's secrets of list-building?

What dieter wouldn't be interested to learn how watching *American Idol* can help in losing weight?

What golfer wouldn't be curious enough to see what the "Captain Jack Sparrow techniques" are?

The point is, there are built-in opportunities to grab attention (and get sales!) by including pop culture lessons as the focus of your small report.

Some examples:

1. *3 Word-Of-Mouth Marketing Lessons From The Academy Awards*
2. *What I Learned From Victoria's Secret About Wooing Women*
3. *The American Idol Fan's Guide To Relationships*
4. *The Survivor Success Model For Achieving Your Dreams*
5. *How To Turn "You're Fired" Into "You're Hired"*
6. *Everything I Know About Dieting I Learned From Shrek*

18. Current Events Tie-In

Another great idea for your next information product is to tie the content to an upcoming holiday or event. The reason this is such an effective report is because it has a natural "urgency" trigger. In other words, the potential customer needs to buy your small report *now* to reap the benefits by the imposed deadline (i.e. the date of the event or holiday).

Some examples:

1. *How To Lose 10 Pounds Before Spring Break*
2. *17 Ways To Save Money On Christmas Gifts*
3. *How To Take The Summer Vacation Of Your Dreams ... For Free*
4. *How To Land The Deal Of a Century At This Year's Convention*
5. *10 Ways To Raise Funds Before April 15th*
6. *The Last-Minute Shopper's Guide For Planning A Great Anniversary*

19. Save Money

There are two big opportunities I feel are missing in most "niche" marketing when it comes to topics for any kind of product (especially "small reports"). First is the "save money" category. The idea here is to create a small report that teaches the reader how to save money or completely eliminate the cost associated with a particular activity.

Think about the appeal of this particular kind of information product:

You're offering the reader the opportunity to reduce (sometimes greatly) the costs associated with something they were going to do anyway!

Who wouldn't pay $10 for your small report if it's going to save them $20, $50, $100 or even more? Who wouldn't pay $10 for your small report if it's going to allow them to reduce their costs *every time* they complete a particular task or participate in a particular activity?

Two words for you: gold mine.

Some examples:

1. *How To Save At Least 25% On Your Grocery Bill*
2. *How To Take A Cruise Without Spending Any Money*
3. *7 "Tricks" For Getting A Homeowner To Lower The Asking Price*
4. *How To Buy A New Car Below The Dealer Invoice*
5. *The Golfer's Guide To Buying Equipment At Wholesale Prices*
6. *5 Sure-Fire Ways To Save Money On Your Home-Schooling*

20. Make Money

The other untapped opportunity is teaching people how to "make money" doing something they are already going to do anyway. Who wouldn't want to make money with their favorite hobby? Who wouldn't be interested in generating cash doing something they enjoy? Who wouldn't want to get paid to do something they are already going to do?

Two more words for you: gold mine.

When you find a passion of your target audience and then deliver an information product that teaches them how to make money from that passion, you're certain to have a hit on your hands.

Some examples:

1. *How To Make Money Selling Baseball Cards On eBay®*
2. *How To Make Money Selling Hard-To-Find Books On eBay®*
3. *How To Write An Info Product About Lowering Your Golf Score*
4. *How To Start A Christian Bookstore With Virtually No Budget*
5. *How To Turn Your Hobby Into An Internet Business*

21. Faster And Easier

The "faster and easier" report is a resource that reveals information to enable the reader to accomplish some task faster and/or easier than they were previously able to do.

Case Study: There are numerous information-based products out there that teach you how to quickly get listed in the search engines. Traditionally this took weeks, even months, to accomplish; now it can be done in days and even hours, based on techniques shared in some of these courses.

Some examples:

1. *7 Ways To Get Faster Results From Your Loan Request*
2. *How To Re-String Your Tennis Racket In Half The time*
3. *The Easiest Way To Get Traffic To Your Web Site*
4. *The Easiest Way To Lose 5 Pounds*
5. *5 Simple Strategies For Reaching Your Goals Faster*
6. *How To Skip A Few Rungs As You Climb The Corporate Ladder*

22. Barriers And Mistakes

With virtually any pursuit in life, there are potential pitfalls and common blunders associated with that pursuit. The old adage is "an ounce of prevention is worth a pound of cure," and there is some truth to that. A properly positioned small report highlighting barriers and mistakes (and how to avoid them!) would be another great option for you to consider.

Case Study: Chuck McCullough created an entire product (not just a "small report") around the concept of common mistakes that affiliate marketers make. It was a hugely popular product upon its release at AffiliateMistakes.com. (I have no affiliation whatsoever, just wanted to mention it as an example.)

Some examples:

1. *7 Common Mistakes Homebuyers Make ... And How To Avoid Them*
2. *10 Most Common Chess Mistakes ... And How To Fix Them*
3. *How To Overcome The 7 Barriers That All New Marketers Face*
4. *The 10 Hidden Barriers To Weight Loss No One Told You About*
5. *7 Barriers To Healthy Relationships ... And How To Overcome Them*
6. *5 Stupid Things People Do When Trying To Fix Their Finances*

Note: Your mini-sales letter is very important for this kind of small report. You'll want to stress how easy it is to make mistakes and what disadvantages the reader will face if they don't apply the strategies you share in the small report.

23. Turn Into

It's almost like magic: take something you've already got and turn it into something much more desirable. That's the idea behind this kind of small report. It's presented in the classic "how-to" format (arranged in chronological steps).

Some examples:

1. *How To Turn 5 Paragraphs Into $500 Month*
2. *How To Turn Your Hobby Into A Thriving Business*
3. *How To Turn An Interview Into A Job*
4. *How To Turn Your Worst Enemy Into Your Best Friend*
5. *How To Turn Your Worship Service Into An Everyday Lifestyle*
6. *How To Turn Your Relationship Into A Lifelong Romance*

24. The 5-Minute Guide

The concept of "5 minutes" carries several highly desirable elements to it:

(a) Relief to a problem can be gained in just a few minutes,

(b) Slight changes that bring desirable results can be made in just a few minutes,

(c) An overview "working knowledge" of a process can be learned in just a few minutes.

With so many of life's activities, we'd like a digest version ... we just want to know, in as few words as possible, how to do it. (Why do you think :08 Minute Abs® was so popular!)

Some examples:

1. *The 5-Minute Guide To Relieving Migraines*
2. *The 5-Minute Guide To Freeing Up Your Time*
3. *The 5-Minute Guide To Burning Extra Calories*
4. *The 5-Minute Guide To Using Your Digital Camera*
5. *The 5-Minute Guide To Influencing Others*
6. *The 5-Minute Guide To Organizing Your Life*

25. Survival

There are times in life when, quite frankly, a solution to a problem isn't possible. Not all marriages can be reconciled, not all financial problems can be solved, and not all heart attacks can be avoided. Sometimes difficult times do come, and they must be dealt with. In the "survival" type of small report, you would teach your readers how to deal with a problem they cannot avoid.

Some examples:

1. *How To Survive Divorce And Learn To Love Again*
2. *How To Survive Bankruptcy And Rebound Financially*
3. *How To Survive A Heart Attack And Live Without Fear*
4. *How To Survive The Can-Spam Law And Still Profit With Email*
5. *How To Survive Menopause Without Destroying Your Relationships*
6. *How To Survive A Church Split And Still Lift Up Christ*

26. Top Picks

With so much information available (we've got more flavors available than a sweatshop on steroids! ☺) it can become difficult knowing what's best. That's why a "top picks" kind of small report is another solid idea for you to develop.

Stated simply, you give your opinion as to what the top picks are within your topic. Obviously it's all about your unique sales proposition in selling the content. There's a big difference between these two small report titles...

- *7 Places To Take Your Spouse In Scotland*
- *7 Romantic Scotland Getaways Almost No One Knows About*

Two words come to mind when I think of this option: Consumer Reports®. They are incredibly popular because people want an unbiased review and recommendation for something they are considering buying.

Some examples:

1. *7 Romantic Scotland Getaways Almost No One Knows About*
2. *How To Spend Your $100 Advertising Budget For Max Results*
3. *The 3 Best Ways To Increase Your Auction Bids*
4. *My Top Tips For Getting Traffic To Any Site*
5. *The Top 10 Ways To Find Anything Using Google.com*

27. Age Specific

The final idea I want to share for you to consider as an option for your next small report is what I call "age specific."

What you would do is develop an information product on a specific topic for a specific age group. Let's face it, you wouldn't deal with a toddler the same way you would a teenager. Different ages require different approaches, which makes this a wonderful way for you to "nichefy" your small report (and in many cases, continue to "graduate" your customers from one report to the next as they or someone they know continues to grow older).

Some examples:

1. *Your Complete Guide To Home-Schooling Any 3 to 8 Year-Old*
2. *Soccer Practice Sessions for Kids 8-12*
3. *How To Retire By Age 35 And Never Work Again*
4. *The Senior Citizen's Guide To Starting An Internet Business*
5. *How To Raise A Strong-Willed Child*
6. *How To Deal With A Strong-Willed Teenager*

Closing thoughts

So there you have 27 ideas for your next (or first) information product, along with 158 title topics you can modify for your own use in coming up with an idea for your next project.

Just as a quick reference, I'm going to insert a section that shares 7 ways you can find specific ideas about *your topic* that you can use in conjunction with the categories we've looked at in this report.

Keep an eye out on ClickBank Marketplace. Products that range in the top 5 positions within a particular category are usually selling very well. I'll give you a quick hint: they wouldn't be selling well if there wasn't interest. Look for categories in the marketplace that are related to your particular target audience and scan through the top 5-6 products listed. You're certain to find some great ideas for your small report right there. (And you might even find a great product to promote as your "back end" - more on this in a future lesson). ClickBank's Marketplace can be found at http://www.clickbank.com/marketplace

Scan the best-sellers list at Amazon.com. Do a search in the books section at Amazon.com for keywords and phrases that are related to your particular market. (i.e., "weight loss"

or "home schooling" or "golf"). You should find a nice list of books ranked in order of popularity. This is another built-in research spot for you - and loaded with great ideas for your next small report.

Search in Google.com to see what topics your "competition" has created products on. Pay attention to those listed on the first page and those who are advertising in the ads on the right side of the screen. These will almost always provide you with numerous ideas for your small report and can potentially be a great starting point for joint venture partnerships in the future.

Look in the market-related forums for "hot topics" that might lend themselves to report ideas. There are forums (or "message boards") for just about every market imaginable. Look for discussions in these forums for ideas. Specifically look for topics where there is a *lot* of discussion (numerous posted messages and replies). Pay special attention to people who are complaining about problems or limitations, for whom you might be able to provide solutions in your small report.

Look in popular article directories for existing interest. Drop by article banks and look at articles related to your market for brainstorming ideas. Pay special attention to the "most viewed" articles, as they are a good indicator of which topics are hot and which topics are not.

Find offline magazines related to your market. Drop by your favorite bookstore or news-stand (or visit Magazines. com online) and look at their articles for small report ideas. This is another tremendous way to find great ideas - especially because you get the benefit of their research. They've already invested time in deciding what to write about, based on their market's interest. You don't need to do this kind of research ... simply write about what they are writing about!

Ask subscribers on a mailing list in your market (either your own opt-in list or one you rent) which topics interest them. It's a simple process: (1) Ask your list members what topics interest them the most. (2) Take the topic that gets the most mentions and write your small report about it. Who better to give you ideas about what to write than those who are most likely to buy the small report upon its completion?!

Two of my favorites from this list are Amazon.com and Magazines.com. Let me quickly share a couple of additional actions that I recommend you take *right now* in relation to these two resources.

Amazon.com. Go to the site and type your keyword(s) into the search box upon your arrival. Browse through all the listings. If you use a broad enough search phrase, you should find *dozens* of listings that will almost certainly cover angles you've never even thought of.

Magazines.com. Visit the site and find the category of listings related to your field of interest. Look at the magazines listed in that category and click on the graphic image of the various magazine covers. You'll see actual covers with real featured articles and contents displayed. You should find many solid ideas just by looking at the cover pictures.

So with all of this, you should have ample ideas to get started working on your next small report!

Recommended Resources

Simple Product Profit Formula. If you can write simple 7-15 page reports, you can make a living from the comfort of your own home, working to your own schedule.

www.SimpleProductProfitFormula.com

Free To Fee. Discover how to EXPERTLY put together free content (or Lead Magnets) which converts more browsers into buyers. After all, If you're going to put your time and effort into publishing and giving away free content why not get the best possible benefit from it?

www.FreeToFee.com

Sales Copy Game Plan. Learning how to write good sales copy is one of the most valuable and profitable skills you can pick up in your business career. Because once you know how to craft irresistible, sizzling sales letters, then you'll have the power to sell anything to anyone! This 50+ page hands-on course, put together from proven sales copy ideas, will give you a step-by-step guide for crafting your very own high-response sales letters.

www.SalesCopyGamePlan.com

Email Marketing Game Plan. If you want your customers to buy from you again and again then you need to keep in regular contact with them by email. The Email Marketing Game Plan will show you how to educate and entertain your readers every time. Maintaining high open rates and click through rates every time you email them.

www.EmailMarketingGamePlan.com

Recommended Resources

Affiliate Traffic Game Plan. If you have a traffic problem, you have a business problem. Here's the amazing no-cost strategy for getting other people in your niche to send you their very best customers. You never have to worry about traffic again when you find other people who are willing to get visitors to your website for you! You can put the exact strategies and emails that the experts use to work for you too.

www.AffiliateTrafficGamePlan.com

Premium Product Profit Formula. Discover how to create your own $97 products in 48 hours or less! Ramp up your sales quickly by creating your own "premium" products in just two days.

www.PremiumProductProfitFormula.com

Unfair Advantage Cheat Sheets. Over 880 pages of fill-in-the-blanks templates, swipe files, case studies, training tutorials and more to make writing anything faster, easier, and better. An essential resource for every content author and business owner.

www.UnfairAdvantageCheatSheets.com

Internet Marketing Training Club. The premium destination offering help and support for internet marketers and product developers. Thousands of pages of articles, tools, techniques and tips as well as hours of video tutorials and content featuring experts at the top of their game.

www.InternetMarketingTrainingClub.com